Jewish-Gentile
COURTSHIPS

An Exploratory Study
of a Social Process

JOHN E. MAYER

The Free Press of Glencoe, Inc.

A DIVISION OF THE CROWELL-COLLIER PUBLISHING COMPANY

For DALE

Preface

THIS BOOK owes a great deal to many people. While I was a graduate student at Columbia University, Kingsley Davis and Robert K. Merton each played a large role in shaping my thinking and in so doing contributed immeasurably to whatever merit this book may have. To Kingsley Davis, I am further indebted both for directing my early research efforts in the area of intermarriage and for encouraging me to go further.

Earlier drafts of the study were read by a number of people. Paul F. Lazarsfeld and Mirra Komarovsky offered helpful advice and many thoughtful criticisms. For their valuable suggestions, I would also like to thank Godfrey W. Cobliner, William J. Goode, Wm. Douglas Kilbourn, Jr., Hubert J. O'Gorman, and Morris Zelditch. Carl S. Shoup, in particular, has helped me in many ways and has been a constant source of encouragement and friendly guidance.

It is a pleasure to acknowledge the editorial assistance of Elaine Cohen. Her talents as an editor and critic have been of immense value.

Clearly, the couples who were interviewed for this study deserve special thanks. By agreeing to be interviewed and sharing with us intimate details of their lives, they made the study possible. In addition, their interest in the subject and cordiality to my wife and myself made easier the task of gathering the data. For my part, I have made every effort to preserve their anonymity: changing names, places, and occasionally other characteristics or circumstances that might conceivably lead to their identification. My gratitude goes also to the many people who aided us in the search for respondents.

Finally, the assistance of my wife, Dale, was invaluable. She did all of the preliminary work connected with contacting the respondents and arranging for interview appointments. In addition, she interviewed all of the wives in the study and provided extensive clerical and editorial assistance.

J. E. M.

Contents

6. The Partner's "Concessions" 101
   The Children's Religious Orientation
   The Children's Social Identity

PARENTAL OPPOSITION

7. The Basis of Parental Opposition 125

8. Parental Efforts to Deal with the Relationship 135

9. The Ineffectiveness of Parental Opposition 151
   The Perceptual Lag of Parents
   *Factors Which Reduced the Impact of
   Parental Opposition*

THE RELUCTANT AND HIS FRIENDS

10. The Role of Friends 179
    The Support of Approving Circles
    *The Influence of Mixed and Disapproving
    Circles*

11. A Review of Our Findings 199

    REFERENCE NOTES 230

    INDEX 239

JEWISH-GENTILE

COURTSHIPS

1 . . . *An Overview of Mate*

Selection

IT IS a commonplace observation that nearly all individuals get married at some point in their lives. Obviously, the course of the individual's life will be shaped by his marital choice; moreover, the kinds of combinations that are formed, in their aggregate number, will have far-reaching implications for society as a whole.

What is considerably less clear is why particular unions occur—why individuals pair off as they do. Popular myths notwithstanding, marriages are not "fated to be." In the current study we are concerned with the conditions that lead certain combinations to form rather than others— or, more precisely, with one small aspect of this very broad topic. However, before turning to our specific problem, an overview of the influences that affect mate selection may be helpful. This will enable us to relate our particular research interests to previous thinking and to clarify our point of departure.

With regard to the marriageable population (i.e., individuals who are looking forward to marriage in the not too distant future), obviously, a marriage cannot occur unless the two partners have met.* At the same time, meetings between prospective partners are not solely a matter of chance, a wholly fortuitous event.[1] To some extent, such encounters between members of the marriageable population are a by-product of environmental conditions. For example, neighborhoods, colleges, churches, places of employment, and a variety of other institutional settings will bring together certain persons rather than others. Thus, other things being equal, two individuals are more likely to meet if they go to the same college than if they attend separate ones.

That these environmental conditions play a role in determining the kinds of encounters that occur can be inferred from the findings of a number of studies. For example, investigations of marriage licenses have demonstrated that —more frequently than would be expected by chance—the partners to a marriage were engaged previously in the same kind of work,[2] or that they lived in close proximity to each other.[3] Of course, these findings do not prove conclusively that propinquitous conditions, as such, were actually responsible for bringing husband and wife together: With reference to residential proximity, the individuals may have met first and moved into the same neighborhood afterward; even if they lived in the same neighborhood to begin with, this factor may not have actually been responsible for their meeting. However, there is a strong basis for suspecting that a good many of these meetings were a direct result of geographic proximity.

To take note of a different kind of environmental factor, specific encounters within a given pool of marriageables will be affected by the size of the various subgroups within the parent population. Other things being equal, the smaller a subgroup, relative to the surrounding population, the more likely are the members of that group to meet mar-

* These comments do not apply to marriages that are contracted through the mails, arranged by brokers, etc.

riageable members of the outside population. Again, this can be inferred from data which reveal that the smaller an ethnic, religious, or racial group, relative to the surrounding population, the greater will be the proportion of subgroup members who contract marriages with outsiders. For example, a relationship of this type has been observed to hold for different racial groups in Hawaii;[4] for Protestants and Catholics who live in Switzerland, and whose relative numbers vary from one canton to the next;[5] and for Jews whose proportionate numbers vary within the provinces of Canada[6] and within the republics of the Soviet Union.[7] No doubt there are also other conditions that explain why the outmarriage rate rises as the size of the subgroup decreases: For one, if they are unable to locate promising marital prospects within their own small subgroup, the members may intentionally look for mates in the outside population. Nevertheless, many marriages can probably be traced back to the fact that certain premarital meetings "just happened."

This is not to imply that individual contacts will be determined entirely by environmental conditions, such as those noted above. Clearly, the actor himself will not be passive throughout this process; he will not stand by listlessly, waiting to see "who will turn up," so to speak. Rather, he will actively seek out those individuals who appeal to him and just as actively remove himself from others. Again, certain persons in the population may influence such meetings by deliberately bringing designated men and women together. Parents may take special steps to make sure their children meet the "right" types; a person's friends may introduce him to certain individuals—and steer him away from others.

Nevertheless, it should be recognized that meeting the person he does meet is not entirely a result of the individual's own volition or even the volition of others. To some degree, it will depend upon the particular members of the opposite sex who happen to be present in his milieu. However, the composition of his milieu, in turn, will depend to some extent upon environmental conditions, such as those mentioned previously. In fact, on occasion, the compartmentalizing influence of the social structure makes it very unlikely that the individual will ever meet the specific type of person he is seeking. To illustrate, a woman who lives in a small town may hope to find a husband whose outlook is "cosmopolitan." But there are probably few such men in her environs to begin with; and those who do fit this description may be attending out-of-state colleges or may have previously migrated to more metropolitan centers. As a result of these and other factors, she may never meet a marriageable male of this type. In short, even though we take into account the actor's predilections and the matchmaking activities of those close to him, the meetings which occur between him and members of the opposite sex must, in some measure, be a by-product of environmental conditions.

Needless to say, while external factors will be responsible for bringing certain persons together, not all of these meetings will eventuate in marriage. Why do some of these couples later find themselves at the altar, whereas others do not? In approaching this problem, we believe it is useful, as a first step, to take into consideration the marital predilections of the two individuals at the time of their initial contact. We can think of the two partners as being potentially capable, to a greater or lesser degree, of satisfying each other's marital requirements. We say "potentially" because neither the man nor the woman will be aware initially of the degree to which the other is actually capable of fulfilling his various demands.

However, to go back a step, it will no doubt be agreed that persons who are looking forward to marriage have some conception of the kind of person they would like to marry.[8] In all likelihood, they will have a great many requirements in mind and will hope to find someone who is a composite of a great many things—someone who has particular attributes, traits, attitudes, interests, etc.; someone who will respond to them in a certain manner; and someone who will satisfy certain of their emotional needs. However, at this point we are not concerned with the nature of their marital preferences, but only with the fact that they are more receptive emotionally to certain types of persons than to others. Indeed, it is hard to conceive of an individual who would merely shrug his shoulders when asked what kind of a person he would like to marry.

With these preliminary remarks in mind (i.e., that when members of the opposite sex meet, they will have certain predilections with respect to their future mate and will be able—potentially—to satisfy each other's demands in varying degrees), let us turn to one of the ways in which the contracting of a marriage has been explained. In trying to account for mate selection, a number of investigators visualize the marital union as stemming from the feelings, needs, wishes, desires, etc., that the man and woman bring into the situation and which were "contained" within them prior to their meeting. In other words, the marriage is considered to derive from the fact that the partners satisfy each other's marital proclivities (whether they are fully aware of their own proclivities or not). While what happens after the actors have met is relevant, it is relevant only insofar as it bears upon what the young people bring into the situation.

For example, psychoanalytical theory conceives of marital choice as being a by-product of the actor's affective relationships with the members of his immediate family. His interaction with parents and siblings, extending over a period of time when he is most impressionable, emotionally speaking, leaves a marked imprint upon him—an imprint of which he may not be aware, but which will lead him to be drawn to particular members of the opposite sex in later life. If his early familial experiences have been gratifying, it is quite possible that he will gravitate toward those who conjure up an image of the parent of the opposite sex. If his experiences have been distressing, he may be attracted to individuals who deviate from this image in certain significant ways. The dynamics of this process need not detain us; the essential point is that members of the psychoanalytic school consider the subject's ultimate marital choice incomprehensible without an understanding of these early relationships and their emotional consequences for the actor.[9]

The theory of complementary needs, which has been spelled out by Winch and his colleagues in some detail, also visualizes marriage as stemming from marital predispositions. In this instance, the subject is viewed as having certain unfulfilled emotional needs—many of which are unrecognized by him—which sensitize him to those who he anticipates will gratify these needs: "In mate selection each individual seeks within his or her field of eligibles [i.e., those who are similar in race, religion, class, etc.] for that person who gives the greatest promise of providing him or her with maximum need gratification."[10] The theory goes on to suggest that those couples whose need patterns are complementary, rather than similar, are more likely to be drawn together:

. . . some needs of one member of a couple may be in actual or potential conflict with corresponding needs in the other member of the couple. To the degree that this condition prevails, it is to be expected that they will come to a falling out, that the probability of a break in the relationship before marriage is high. . . . On the other hand . . . the needs of one member may complement the needs of the other. To the degree that this is true, it is anticipated that the affectional bond would be strengthened, that the couple would feel "in love," that the relationship would endure.[11]

However fruitful such predispositional theories may be in accounting for the formation of marriages, they leave a number of questions unanswered.* That predispositional theories, whatever their orientation, fail to provide complete explanations becomes immediately apparent when we recognize that not all of the meetings which occur between individuals who are capable—at least, theoretically—of fulfilling each other's demands eventuate in marriage. In short, such approaches do not explain those instances where couples who might very well be "right" for each other separate soon after meeting, or at least before reaching the altar. This whole category of relationships has tended to slip out of view. We are thus confronted with the question as to why certain couples who are potentially able to gratify each other's demands wind up at the altar, whereas others do not. The same question can be asked with regard to couples where one or both of the members are potentially unable (roughly speaking) to satisfy each other's marital predilections. Why do some of these couples get married, whereas others do not?

Our purpose here has been to bring to the forefront what is a truism (at least to sociologists), namely, that what happens between two persons after they meet cannot be wholly predicted from a knowledge of their predispositions. In other words, although we may know a great deal about the marital requirements of a man and a woman, the outcome of their relationship will nonetheless remain indeterminant to a degree. We cannot know, with any certainty, whether they will become emotionally involved, or react indifferently, or even with dislike, to each other. Whatever course the relationship takes, it must, in some measure, be dependent upon what might be called post-contact or on-going influences.

* This is inevitable, of course, since no theory can hope to be all-encompassing: In concentrating on particular elements in the situation, the investigator must of necessity overlook or pay small heed to other factors.

Let us pause for a moment to illustrate what we mean by "on-going influences." Human interaction involves communication and, as Kingsley Davis has pointed out, "The essential feature of communication is that one person infers from the behavior of another (whether speech, gesture, or posture) what idea or feeling the other is trying to convey. He then reacts not to the behavior as such but to the inferred idea or feeling."[12] As a result, it is always possible that one interactor will ascribe motivations and intentions to the other which do not exist in fact. Consequently, those who are ill-suited, in terms of marital predisposition, may be drawn together, at least for a time, if either one draws invalid inferences about the other, if, in short, one imagines that the other is an essentially different type of person. Conversely, a warm relationship between those who are potentially well-suited may never develop. An affective attachment may be forestalled, or derailed if it does get under way, because one or both subjects have drawn faulty inferences with regard to the other.

Moreover, even when they are correct in their inferences, the feeling tone that emerges will not simply be an outgrowth of what both "bring into the situation." Social relationships, whether they are friendly or cool, do not develop in a vacuum. In all likelihood, the course of the affair will also be affected by the partners' on-going relationships with other significant members of their environment. How others, such as parents and friends, feel about the affair inwardly, and how they react outwardly, will presumably make a difference.°

With the exception of Willard Waller, who has so perceptively depicted the interaction of men and women in

---

° In their study of engaged couples, Ernest W. Burgess and Paul Wallin found a high correlation between parental opposition and broken engagements. When at least one of the four parents disapproved of the marriage, 25 per cent of the couples (55 out of 218) broke their engagements. When parents on both sides approved, only 11 per cent of the couples (74 out of 666) broke their engagements.[13]

the courtship setting,[14] it would appear that the entire area of post-contact influences has remained relatively untouched. However, there is reason to believe that on-going influences are of great importance in explaining the formation of marriages. Furthermore, in our opinion, it would very definitely be a step in the right direction if these influences were considered in conjunction with the marital predilections of the individuals concerned. In other words, we might first classify couples in terms of the degree to which each partner was potentially capable of satisfying the other's requirements. Categorizing them very crudely at this point, we might regard the two partners as being either well-suited or ill-suited in terms of their predispositions. We might then ask: What are the on-going influences which lead certain couples of each type to get married, whereas others do not?

The Choice of an Ineligible Mate

Identification of the factors which lead an individual to marry someone he formerly considered ineligible constituted the focus of our study. More generally, we wished to investigate those elements which are responsible for marriages between individuals who are predispositionally ill-suited to each other.

As he looks ahead to marriage, we know that the actor will hope to find someone who represents his ideal in many respects. However, certain factors may be of such vital importance to him that unless members of the opposite sex can fulfill these requirements, they will automatically be eliminated as matrimonial possibilities. For example, a young man may feel that it is inconceivable—or at least highly unlikely—that he could ever marry someone who was ten years his senior; or someone who hadn't graduated from grammar school; or someone who was physically disabled, excessively domineering, or totally devoid of humor. Nevertheless, at some future date he may find himself wedded to just such a person. On some occasions, after he has actually met a woman with one or more of these "undesirable" characteristics, he may discover that his feelings toward her are not what he had expected. Certain other characteristics may impress him very favorably. When he appraises her as a whole person, and not solely in terms of her "liability," he may no longer feel—or at least not as strongly—that she would be an unacceptable mate. On the other hand, he may continue to feel—and for some time— that she would be a wholly unsuitable marital choice. In any event, if he does marry her, the man will have chosen a partner in a manner that was inconsistent—at least partially inconsistent—with his earlier marital predilections.

The question arises as to the nature of the on-going influences which lead an individual to make a marital choice of this type. What influences were operating in the case of our young man that were absent in the case of other individuals who also met ineligibles but who never became affectively attached to them?

As will be recognized, this problem is not confined to instances of marital choice; it has relevance for other types of affective relationships as well. For example, there are people who feel they could not possibly associate with Negroes, or Catholics, or homosexuals. Yet, at some point in the future, they may well enter into friendly relations with such individuals. When we view this phenomenon at the level of the group, many diverse instances come to mind in which affective ties develop between those who are members (and, moreover, nonalienated members) of groups that are mutually opposed. For example, friendships are not unknown to occur between soldiers in the forces of the occupation and embittered members of the vanquished country; between sophisticated summer transients on vacation and "standoffish" members of the provincial population; or between pre-adolescent boys and girls, each of whose cliques views members of the opposite sex as anathema.

While our own immediate focus is on marriage, the processes leading to marriage are not wholly dissimilar from those which lead to friendship. Perhaps, then, in the course of our study, we shall also be able to shed further light on the influences that lead persons to become friendly with those individuals they had formerly considered ineligible, i.e., as "unfit" for intimate association.*

* Insofar as sociologists and social psychologists have been concerned with the manner in which on-going influences affect the formation of social relationships, they have tended to dwell upon friendships, *per se*, rather than marriages.[15] However, these and other writings have a bearing on, or are directly responsible for, cetain points we hope to develop.

2 . . . *The Nature of the Study*

TO EXPLORE the problem outlined above, we tried to find Jewish and Gentile subjects who had been intent upon contracting an ingroup marriage, but who subsequently married outside of their group. The decision to focus on Jews and Gentiles—rather than on individuals who had married someone of the "wrong" age, for example, or with the "wrong" looks—grew out of an earlier interest in mixed marriages.*

More important, there was reason to believe that Jews and Gentiles of the type we sought would make particularly appropriate subjects. It is well known that there is marked resistance to such marriages; presumably, the more anxious our subjects were to avoid becoming involved with a certain type of person, the more clearly would the influences which promoted their "involvement" be revealed. In short, if our subjects were strongly, rather than weakly, motivated to reject a particular type of individual, the conditions re-

* In a previous study, with objectives quite different from the current one, an effort was made to account for the prevailing rates and patterns of Jewish-Christian marriages in this country.[1]

sponsible for their marital choice would be more apparent to any outside observer.*

Although this information is probably familiar, let us briefly review certain facts which indicate the presence of intermarriage resistance on the part of large sectors of the population. It is common knowledge that the cultural norms to which Jews, Protestants, and Catholics are exposed prescribe that marriages should be contracted only within the group; marriages with outsiders are not sanctioned. Among the Jews, for example, intermarriage has traditionally been looked upon with abhorrence. Historically speaking, it was considered a catastrophe, something to be avoided at all costs. The outmarrying Jew was branded a renegade by the community and was considered dead by his parents, who even sat *shiva*† for him. Although they may not be as intense today, such sentiments have persisted and are still characteristic of some Jewish families.[2]

Moreover, the religious spokesmen for these groups—rabbis, priests, and ministers—have not failed to express themselves strongly on the subject. As is well known, members of the clergy are unequivocally opposed to mixed marriages. In fact, the large majority will refuse to perform such a marriage, unless, of course, the other partner converts or agrees to certain stipulations—for example, with regard to the religious training of the children.[3]

As might be expected, attitude surveys have revealed no great readiness on the part of young people to become a partner to such a marriage. Thus, when Jewish adolescents in Riverton (a pseudonym for an eastern industrial city) were asked how they would feel about marrying a non-

* The fact that Jewish-Gentile marriages are heterogamous does not mean, of course, that homogamous marriages would necessarily have been inappropriate for studying the problem we have outlined. For example, individuals who had been very anxious to marry someone of a higher social class, but who later married at their own social level, would have constituted suitable subjects.

† A period of mourning for the dead.

Jew, seven out of ten indicated that "they wouldn't like it," and many of the others were "uncertain."[4] In a national survey of high school students, 52 per cent of the Protestants and 59 per cent of the Catholics indicated they would not consider marrying a Jew.[5]

Finally, the resistance of Jews and Christians to intermarriage can be inferred from the fact that relatively few such marriages have been contracted within our society. Previously, this was revealed by the sundry findings of scattered community surveys;[6] only recently have statistical data become available for the entire population. In March 1957, for the first time, the Bureau of the Census asked a nation-wide sample of the population to state their religion (on a voluntary basis). Among other things, the results revealed that for every ninety-three marriages in which both partners were Jewish, there were only seven in which one of the partners was Jewish and the other was not.[7]

Methodology

OBTAINING THE SUBJECTS

One of the chief problems confronting us was how to find intermarried persons who had been negatively predisposed to such a marriage. From the outset, we felt fairly confident we could locate mixed couples, *per se,* by asking others, such as acquaintances or clergymen, to provide us with the names of such persons. However, there was a good chance that this kind of indiscriminate procedure might lead us to interviewees who were inappropriate subjects for our study. For these individuals might very well have been unconcerned as to whether their mates were Jewish or Gentile; in fact, they may have been anxious to cross ethnic lines.

Persons of this description are, in fact, more likely to show up in a study of intermarriage if one is not selective.

At least this is suggested by the types of intermarried spouses who have "appeared" in other investigations. For example, in a study of Jewish-Gentile marriages in Chicago, husbands and wives were classified as follows: emancipated, rebellious, detached, adventurous, promiscuous, marginal, acculturated, and unorganized (or demoralized).[8] These thumb-nail descriptions suggest that these subjects were not resistant to the idea of marrying out of their group. Again, in another investigation involving Negro-white marriages, recently married couples were categorized as follows: intellectuals and "Bohemians"; religious and political radicals; members of the "sporting world"; and the stable middle class (only a small proportion fell into this group).[9]

Thus, we realized that it was essential that we ascertain in advance the premarital attitudes of our prospective subjects toward intermarriage. At the same time, however, we felt we could not obtain this information unless we actually interviewed them. We did not expect—and rightly so, as it turned out—that, as a rule, our intermediaries would know the prospective interviewees well enough to provide us with information of this nature. Moreover, it seemed to us that this was not the kind of material that could be obtained easily or tactfully in a short preliminary interview, whether this interview took the form of a telephone conversation, a written questionnaire, or a personal meeting.

However, we felt there was a partial solution to this dilemma—namely, that there was more likelihood of obtaining appropriate subjects if we secured only the names of couples whose parents (either one or both sets) had been strongly opposed to the marriage. We reasoned that individuals with parents of this description would have been more reluctant to cross ethnic lines than would those individuals whose parents had been "lukewarm" or accepting.

At the same time, we were well aware that this method

provided no guaranty that we would be put in touch with the kind of persons we were seeking. For one thing, our intermediary might simply have misjudged the extent of parental disapproval. And even if his assessment was correct, this was no assurance that the subject would meet our criteria. The subject might have been indifferent to his parents' opposition. And if he did care about his parents' opinions, he still might not be negatively predisposed to intermarriage in an over-all sense. Other elements in the situation might have led him to view intermarriage with favor, and these elements might have counteracted the deterring influence of his parents. However uneconomical our solution to the problem of obtaining appropriate respondents may appear, it seemed the most feasible alternative at the time.*

With this plan in mind, in the spring of 1954 we began to solicit the names of mixed couples in the New York metropolitan area. In addition to the "parental opposition" requirement, we sought only the names of couples who had been married recently (approximately five years or less), for we felt that the more recent the marriage, the more fully would the subject be able to recall the events which surrounded his courtship. Since we were interested in the *kinds* of influences that operate to produce such marriages, rather than their *distribution* in a universe of mixed couples, no effort was made to obtain a representative sample.† Instead, we tried to secure couples from as many different walks of life as possible. It was reasoned that this greater diversification in background would produce a greater variety of influences for investigation. Finally, in addition to

---

* Since then, we have concluded that if one must select his subjects "blindly," one might do better to seek out unions in which one of the partners converted to the other's faith before the marriage. The nonconverted member might very well turn out to be an appropriate subject, based on the reasoning that it was his resistance to intermarriage that led the other to convert.

† Needless to say, anyone who wished to obtain such a sample would be confronted with formidable difficulties.

the group described above, we tried to locate individuals who had been engaged to (or seriously interested in) cross-ethnics, but who broke off the relationship solely (or at least primarily) because of their resistance to intermarriage. Such persons would have constituted an appropriate control group, enabling us to make comparisons between individuals whose predispositions were similar, but whose subsequent romances took a different course. However, the task of locating such subjects proved to be hopelessly difficult and the attempt was given up fairly early in the study.

Efforts were made to secure the names of mixed couples in a number of different ways. We asked acquaintances if they knew any such couples personally, or whether such individuals were known to them indirectly. We made the same request of rabbis, ministers, and priests, and of college students in New York City. Finally, we asked the intermarried couples we interviewed for the names of other such couples.

We encountered no obstacle in obtaining the names of intermarried couples, *per se;* but it frequently turned out that the only couple (or couples) the intermediary could think of had received the blessings of both sets of parents. The intermarried persons who were called to our attention were apt to be well-educated, cosmopolitan, and wholly indifferent to ethnic considerations. Thus, the mere task of securing the names of individuals who fulfilled our requirements turned out to be time-consuming and laborious. We had felt that once we had enlisted the aid of a good many intermediaries, we would be able to locate additional subjects without too much difficulty, that there would be a kind of snowball effect, so to speak. Unfortunately, this did not turn out to be the case.

When we finally did secure the names of couples who fit our criteria, we wrote each a letter, requesting an interview. The letter explained, in a very general way, that we were interested in the conditions which lead to mixed marriages; and, of course, the name of the intermediary who had referred the couple to us was mentioned. If they were willing to participate in the study, an appointment was made to talk with them at their home. At that time, the husband and wife were interviewed simultaneously, but in separate rooms.* The session generally lasted about two and one-half hours; during this time, we tried to write down as much of what was said as we could. Typically, the couples were very hospitable, and at the end of the interview we frequently stayed on for a short visit. This is pertinent, because once the interview paraphernalia was out of the way and everyone felt more relaxed, there was a tendency for the couples to "open up" more; as a result, we were occasionally supplied with additional interesting material.

THE CHARACTERISTICS OF OUR SUBJECTS

Our interest in the current study naturally centers on those of our subjects who had been resistant to crossing ethnic lines in marriage, and we shall shortly describe the method by which we identified these individuals. However, we have not totally ignored the remaining interviewees; we have made use of them in certain supplementary ways, particularly in the section of our study which deals with parents and children.

At this point, some facts about the composition of the group as a whole would seem to be in order.

1. There were 45 couples in the group, 3 of whom were engaged. However, the total number of persons interviewed was 86 and not 90 (as it would have been, if both members had been interviewed in every case). One of the husbands refused to participate in the study. The three other exceptions involved the engaged couples; in each instance,

* I interviewed the men; my wife interviewed the women.

one of the partners was out of town and therefore unavailable.

2. The names of the couples were obtained through the following channels: 16 came from our acquaintances or from acquaintances of theirs; 10 from rabbis and 3 from priests; 8 from college students; 8 from the couples who were subsequently interviewed.

3. In 33 combinations, the husband was Jewish and the wife was Gentile (19 Jewish-Protestant, 14 Jewish-Catholic). In 12 cases, the husband was Gentile and the wife was Jewish (7 Catholic-Jewish, 5 Protestant-Jewish).*

4. This was primarily a middle-class group. For example, at the time of marriage, two-fifths of the husbands were professionals or were training for a profession. The remaining three-fifths were evenly distributed among the following occupational categories: owners of small businesses or executives; salesmen or clerical workers; skilled or unskilled workers. In terms of education, two-thirds of these men and women had at least some college education, and one-half of the group had college degrees.

5. It was a first marriage for 9 out of 10 of these individuals. At the time of marriage the median age of the husbands was 26; the median age of the wives was 23.

6. The couples in our study had been married recently. Four out of 5 had been married for 3 years or less; with one exception, they had all been married less than 7 years.

IDENTIFICATION OF THE RELUCTANTS

In order to ascertain the orientation of our subjects with regard to intermarriage prior to meeting their mates, we asked a number of direct questions. Early in the interview —but only after we felt that some rapport had been estab-

---

* As can be seen, about three times as many couples fall into the first category. This numerical inequality is not atypical. Statistics from different parts of the world consistently reveal that intermarriages of the first type are more common.[10]

lished—we asked them to recall their earlier feelings about becoming a partner to such a marriage. Then, to gain further information—and to provide a check on their responses—essentially the same question, clothed in different form, was raised again. At this point, the interviewees were asked to describe how they had felt, after the meeting with their future mates had occurred, about becoming involved with a person who was Jewish (or Christian).

On the basis of their responses to these questions—taken in conjunction with certain of their offhand remarks and remarks which were made about them by their partners— we feel reasonably confident that 29 of these persons had been resistant to intermarriage, in the sense that the forces which pushed them away from such a marriage were considerably greater than those which would lead them in that direction. We have labeled these individuals "Reluctants," in contrast to the "Amenables" who constituted the remaining subjects. Our Reluctants consisted of 10 Jewish women, 9 Gentile women, 7 Jewish men, and 3 Gentile men, representing 25 couples. We have categorized these 25 couples in Table 1, in terms of the predisposition toward intermarriage of both partners: *

Table 1. Predisposition toward Intermarriage

	Number of Couples
Jewish husband—Gentile wife	
Both partners Reluctant	1
Husband Reluctant—wife Amenable	6
Wife Reluctant—husband Amenable	8
Gentile husband—Jewish wife	
Both partners Reluctant	3
Husband Reluctant—wife Amenable	0
Wife Reluctant—husband Amenable	7
Total	25

To bring the Reluctants' earlier attitudes toward intermarriage into sharper focus, a few excerpts from their in-

* When the Reluctant's partner was not interviewed (two instances), he was arbitrarily categorized as an Amenable.

terviews have been reproduced below. About one-half of
the Reluctants had been adamantly opposed to intermarriage:

[JEWISH WIFE]: I certainly was hesitant about becoming involved with a non-Jewish person. . . . I never thought of going
out with Jack, because I had avoided going out with non-Jews
all the time. When I had a blind date, and the boy turned out
to be non-Jewish, I didn't go out with him again, even if he was
nice.

[CATHOLIC WIFE]: How did my parents feel about the Jews?
[*Respondent made a sound indicating disgust and revulsion.*]
It was the worst insult they could say, to say to someone—
"You're like a Jew!" All of my family felt this way. . . . I was very
influenced by their opinions. Actually, I think I felt almost
stronger than they did about Jews. . . . I never had any thoughts
about mixed marriages before I met my husband, because I
simply wouldn't go out with a Jewish person. . . . As for marrying
a Jew, that was simply unheard of!

[JEWISH HUSBAND]: [*Before you met your wife, do you recall if
you had any thoughts about mixed marriages?*] Oh yes, definitely! I remember that my best friend in medical school married a Gentile girl. I thought she was a nice girl right along, but
that I would not do anything like that! . . . Also, I remember a
guy from the block who married a girl from Texas. I remember
wondering why he would do anything like that. I felt it was a
stupid thing to do, it was just something that was not done. . . .
Yes, I felt very hesitant about becoming involved with my wife,
and this feeling lasted until I was married.

Others, while resistant, had been less strongly opposed
to intermarriage; and there were a few who were only
mildly opposed:

[JEWISH HUSBAND]: I had decided that if a girl were Gentile,
but she fit the description of what I wanted, religion would not
stand in the way. I say this with a slight reservation. I did have

certain hesitations. I would think more about it. I would make sure there were certain compensations.

The Reluctants' outlook emerges with even greater clarity when we review the comments of a few of their opposite number—the Amenables. The latter had felt little or no resistance to crossing ethnic lines:

[CATHOLIC WIFE]: I felt absolutely nothing about the Jews while I was growing up. Maybe that's peculiar, but I never knew any. . . . Occasionally, I remember hearing my parents tell an anti-Semitic joke, but they were certainly few and far between. . . . I did have some thoughts about intermarriage before I met my husband, but I can honestly say I never paid much attention to the difference in religion. When I was growing up, people's religion was never impressed upon us. We were told that the important thing was a person's personality. . . . I knew there was a possibility that I might intermarry because I was going out with people of different religions, but I never thought about it. It wouldn't have made any difference.

[PROTESTANT WIFE]: I remember one of my mother's favorite expressions was that she had a Jewish streak down her back. [*What did she mean by that?*] I can tell you better what she meant by the way she acted. She was highly belligerent against the Germans during the war because of their persecution of the Jews. My mother was deeply religious. She used to say that the Germans would get their just reward for their maltreatment of the chosen people, meaning the Jews. . . . I would say that most of the people where we lived in Texas, if they thought at all about the Jews, thought they were merchants, tightwads, and rich. This isn't surprising because the few Jews they saw were usually like that . . . merchants who had settled in the small towns. As for how my friends in high school felt about the Jews, the question never came up. That's the way it was for me, except that if someone had made me say something about the Jews, I probably would have had the feelings my mother had, because they were the only ones I ever heard expressed.

[JEWISH WIFE]: I was in favor of mixed marriages. I always felt more comfortable with people who were not Jewish. I don't know why—it just happened that way. . . . I guess I anticipated I might marry someone of a different religion, because after my first marriage was annulled I went out with anyone, regardless of their religion. It made no difference to me what their religion was. I had thought about it, and it still made no difference. . . . No, I didn't feel hesitant about becoming involved with my husband because he was non-Jewish. This was because my upbringing was completely irreligious. My family had never stressed any of the Jewish traditions or clannishness.

[JEWISH HUSBAND]: Yes, I had some thoughts about mixed marriages before meeting my wife. I thought it was a good thing. I liked it because it was an indication that people didn't care. [*Did you anticipate that you might marry out of your group?*] Yes, quite often. I was very preoccupied with this whole issue and had many debates with myself about it. I would say to myself that it would be nice to marry a Gentile girl—it would be an indication that I had put certain phony values behind me. It would be an indication that I was more mature. . . . On the other hand, I felt I would be more at home with a Jewish girl. . . . There was a kind of schism in my thinking, I was pulled in opposite directions.

We cannot be absolutely certain, of course, that every one of the individuals we have labeled as a Reluctant was, in fact, negatively predisposed toward outmarrying before he met his spouse or, conversely, that all of the Amenables had been agreeable to marrying someone of a different religious affiliation. For one thing, the interviewee's precontact sentiments may have been colored by his experiences over the succeeding years. As a result, the account he provided of his feeling may have failed to coincide with his actual feelings at the time. In brief, there may have been a discrepancy between the actual situation in the past and his current report. Moreover, the topic touched on sensitive areas. Some of our subjects appeared ill-at-ease when it was broached and were hesitant about communicating their feelings. It was our impression that Christians who had not wanted to outmarry and Jews who had wanted to cross ethnic lines were particularly uncomfortable when questioned about their predispositions. Perhaps the former believed that if they expressed their feelings, this would be taken as a sign that they were anti-Semitic. As for Jews who were anxious to outmarry, they may have believed their marital choice would be regarded as an attempt to detach themselves from their background. For that reason, they may have felt their marriage would be looked upon as not quite authentic—in the manner in which the feelings of an impoverished husband for his wealthy wife are occasionally subject to question. In any event, it is possible that some of these persons disguised their true feelings. Finally, if we assume that the respondent was able to recall his feelings with accuracy and was willing to convey them, were these his "true" feelings? Or were his "real" sentiments wholly or partially unrecognized by him? Short of a psychiatric screening, there is no way to answer this question accurately; in no sense, was the kind of interview we employed designed to uncover unconscious motivations.

However, we did submit a number of standardized questions to all our subjects, regarding certain aspects of their background and their courtship. If we have correctly separated the Reluctants from the Amenables, we might reasonably expect these two subgroups to differ in certain ways. Since, as is evidenced below, they do in fact differ, these data lend additional support to our initial categorization. Specific differences between the two subgroups are summarized below.

1. The Jewish Reluctants in our group were more affirmatively oriented toward their Jewish identity than were the Jewish Amenables. This was evidenced (among other ways) in their answers to the following question: "Let us

suppose that when you were 19 or 20, you had been given the opportunity of being born over again. Would you have preferred to be Jewish or Gentile in your "second life"? (See Table 2.)

Table 2. Choice of Identity of Jewish Subjects

	Reluctants	Amenables
Would have preferred to be Jewish	93%	32%
No preference	7	26
Would have preferred to be Gentile	0	42
	100%	100%
Number of respondents	(15)	(19)

2. The Reluctants had fewer friends in the other ethnic group and dated such individuals less frequently than did the Amenables. (See Tables 3 and 4.)

Table 3. Ethnic Affiliation of Friends of the Same Sex When Respondent Was Past High School Age

	Reluctants	Amenables
Friends in the same ethnic group as respondent	54%	44%
Friends half Jewish, half Gentile	39	30
Friends ethnically different from respondent	7	26
	100%	100%
Number of respondents	(28)	(54)

Table 4. Ethnic Affiliation of Dating Partners When Respondent Was Past High School Age

	Reluctants	Amenables
Dating partners in the same ethnic group as respondent	75%	43%
Dating partners half Jewish, half Gentile	11	26
Dating partners ethnically different from respondent	14	31
	100%	100%
Number of respondents	(28)	(51)

Moreover, of those who had at least one serious romance before meeting their mates, 18 per cent (3 out of 17) of the

Reluctants had been involved with a cross-ethnic, as compared to 54 per cent (20 out of 37) of the Amenables.*

3. The Reluctants' parents were more apt to be opposed to the marriage. This conclusion is based on the replies made by the subjects to the following questions: "How much opposition did your mother (father) feel upon learning that you were serious: none; very little; some, but not much; a fair amount; a good deal; or a great deal?" (See Table 5.)

4. Finally, the courtships of those couples in which one or both of the partners was a Reluctant, compared to those in which neither was a Reluctant, differed in the following ways:

(a) The former group had longer courtships. For them, the median length of time from their meeting until their marriage was 21 months; for the latter group, it was 15 months.

* A number of these Amenables stated that their earlier dating and romantic experiences with cross-ethnics were responsible, at least in part, for their willingness to outmarry. However, of particular interest are the following remarks by a Catholic girl of Polish descent, who came from an extremely anti-Semitic background: "Earlier, when I had been hesitant about going out with Jews, I had been in . . . a parochial school. I had never known any Jews and had led a sheltered life. When I went into nurses' training, I was away from home and living at the hospital most of the time. . . . *At the hospital there were only a few Jewish doctors, but they were the outstanding ones, and everyone admired them. It was easy to have romantic fantasies about these people.* . . . After I was through with nurses' training, I wouldn't have refused to go out with anyone because he was Jewish. It wouldn't have constituted a problem for me." Possibly, the "admiration" which "everyone" accorded these Jewish doctors was a by-product of the fact that Jews tend to be excluded from medical schools.[11] As a result, only those who are especially well qualified, or are considered meritorious on other grounds, are apt to be admitted. In turn, the very "superiority" of such Jews may be instrumental in undermining the prejudices of those with whom they come into contact. One wonders, for example, if the nurse quoted above would have had "romantic fantasies" (in view of her background), if she had been confronted with "average" Jews. It is ironic that by admitting only "superior" members of minority groups—whether Negroes, Puerto Ricans, Italians, etc.—professional schools, business organizations, social clubs, etc. may create a situation which reduces the prejudice of other members of the organization. Of course, this is not inevitable; instead, the minority member may be looked upon as an exception.[12]

Table 5. Parental Opposition

	Reluctants' Parents*	Amenables' Parents*
Not opposed	9%	53%
Mildly or moderately opposed	32	15
Strongly opposed	59	32
	100%	100%
Number of sets of parents	(22)	(43)

* Separate ratings for mother and father were combined to form an average.

(b) More of the couples in the first group broke off the relationship at some point in the premarital stage, namely, 1 out of 3, as compared to 1 out of 5 of those couples in which both members were Amenables. (Usually, these separations lasted for only about a week.)

The bases of the Reluctants' aversion to intermarriage are of particular interest. However, since we will be returning to this topic, we will discuss it only briefly at this juncture. For one thing, the Reluctants knew how their parents would react. Since their parents' feelings were important to them, their desire not to antagonize them is quite understandable. Typically, they commented as follows:

[JEWISH WIFE]: [*Why did you feel you wouldn't marry someone of a different religion?*] I didn't want to hurt my mother, who was against my marrying out of my religion.

[JEWISH WIFE]: Yes, I felt hesitant about becoming involved with a non-Jewish person. It was mostly because of my family. I knew they'd be against it.

Quite apart from their expectations as to how their parents would react, many had felt varying degrees of "inner" resistance. They had been raised within the religious-cultural traditions of their group; they had assimilated these group values and were anxious to perpetuate them in their own marriage. In addition, several indicated that they had not been impervious to differences in social standing:

[PROTESTANT HUSBAND]: I had . . . an emotional block against intermarriage. I had the feeling that people of Catholic or Jewish faiths were just not as good as Protestants. I had a feeling of superiority as a Protestant and a feeling that marrying a Jew or a Catholic would involve loss of status. It would be socially embarrassing.

Other Gentiles, while they themselves may not have looked down on the Jews, had been sensitive to what they felt would be the reactions of others:

[PROTESTANT WIFE]: I remember a Jewish boy asked me for a date once, and I refused because they had their own groups that they went with. I wasn't sure of how my friends and family would feel about it, but I thought they probably would not like it. I felt hesitant because of how people feel about the Jews.

The Design of the Study

Our purpose in interviewing these intermarried persons —who we hoped would turn out to be Reluctants—was to try to uncover some of the influences leading to their marriages. However, since the factors which influence an individual's marital choice are infinite in number, and just as diverse in character, it was necessary to make some initial decisions as to which aspects of this process we would focus on and how thoroughly we would study any given aspect.

From the outset, we decided to explore a wide range of influences, rather than a more circumscribed range in a more intensive manner. With this goal in view, the Reluctant's marital decision was visualized, not only as a function of what had happened between himself and his partner, but also as a function of his relationships with his parents and friends. While it was inevitable that his feelings would have been dependent primarily upon his partner, *per se,* we felt the romance might also have been affected by the nature of his interaction with members of his primary environment. To repeat, instead of confining ourselves to what went on between the principals, we decided to extend our inquiry into a wider range of influences. Obviously, such a decision means that one cannot devote very much attention to any given facet of the courtship; on the whole, the material gathered will, therefore, be relatively superficial. On the other hand, a wider focus may serve to call attention to certain influences which are worthy of further investigation but which might not come to light in a more intensive study.

Accordingly, on the basis of our earlier thinking on this subject, along with clues provided in the literature, we drew up a schedule which dealt with the Reluctant's relationship with his partner, his parents, and his friends. Within these three sets of relationships, the subject's attention was directed to certain topics and areas which we felt might be relevant. In a few instances, we had certain hypotheses in mind, generally derived from ideas which had been expressed in the literature; when this was the case, we deliberately drew the respondent out along these lines. In other instances, we merely had vague ideas or "hunches," so to speak, many of which were abandoned and replaced by others as we went along. However, by and large, we had few specific preconceptions as to the influences which might have been operating. For this reason, among others, we invariably encouraged the interviewees to talk about those factors they personally felt were important—factors which we might not have considered otherwise. As we proceeded, and as certain lines of inquiry seemed unproductive and other more promising ones emerged, our schedule was modified accordingly.

There are, of course, numerous limitations to a study such as this; we shall mention a few of the more important ones at this point. For one thing, it is quite clear that whether one aims at breadth or depth, one can secure only a very incomplete picture of the forces which determined an individual's marital choice in the course of a single interview. A host of influences are involved—some subtle, some not so subtle; some of brief duration, others of longer duration; some clearly recognized, others only dimly perceived. In all probability, it would be possible to obtain a relatively complete account of the factors responsible for an individual's marital choice only if the subject had kept a detailed diary of his feelings, thoughts, and experiences throughout his courtship.

Again, as mentioned earlier, because we tried to cover a lot of territory, we were only able to scratch the surface of any given facet of the courtship process. We could not stop and ask further questions because of the limited amount of time at our disposal. As a result, our discussion will be relatively crude and oversimplified. The reader will find few of the subtle nuances which are contained, for instance, in Waller's depictions of the way young people interact in the courtship setting.

Finally, we are dealing with a very small group of cases. However, despite these limitations, we believe that it is still possible to shed some light on the influences leading to the type of marital choice with which we are concerned. In an effort to achieve this objective, we shall (a) identify some of the conditions responsible for the Reluctant's marital decision; (b) call attention to other factors which we suspect may have played a role in such decisions; and (c) raise a number of questions which we believe merit further consideration.

In summary, we have looked upon the Reluctant's marital

decision as stemming from his relationship with his partner, his parents, and his friends. While his attachment to his partner was certainly a crucial factor in this decision, the course of his affair also depended (in varying degrees) on his interaction with other significant members of his environment. Moreover, the various influences which affected his romance were operative simultaneously. That is, at any given stage in the courtship, his feelings for his partner were the resultant of the three sets of relationships in which he was involved. Obviously, we cannot consider all of these at the same time. If it is to become manageable, the concrete reality of the situation must be broken down into segments. Accordingly, the study has been divided into the following sections: In the first section, we shall focus upon the Reluctant's relationship with his partner. In the second, we shall turn to his relationship with his parents.* In the final section, we shall consider the Reluctant's relationships with his friends.

* For reasons to be explained later, in this section we have augmented the size of the group to include some of the Amenables.

THE RELUCTANT AND
HIS PARTNER

3 . . .   *Initial Phases of the*

Relationship

WE CAN better understand why the Reluctant became emotionally involved with his partner if we subdivide this developmental process into several stages. Roughly, at the first stage, the Reluctant met his partner; at a later point, he became "interested"; finally, he became "involved." Clearly, this process might never have been initiated—and once it was initiated, it might have been arrested at a later point. In other words, it was not inevitable that the Reluctant would meet his partner; having met, it was not inevitable that he would become interested; having become interested, it was not inevitable that he would become involved. In this section of our study, after describing how the partners met, we shall trace some of the influences which led the Reluctant's feelings to move from one plateau to the next.

The Meeting

Over half of the Reluctants in our group met their future mates within various institutional settings; the rest met their partners through friends. The "institutional" couples met in the course of their education, or because they worked together, or because they were members of the same social club. In addition, public recreational facilities, e.g., bowling alleys, ice-skating rinks, etc., were instrumental in bringing a few of these dyads together. These organizational settings differed in certain ways; as a result, some promoted the romance more than others. For one thing, they differed in terms of how frequently they brought the young persons into the same setting. Public recreational facilities brought them together once, but did not necessarily bring them together again in the future. On the other hand, schools, places of employment, and social clubs drew the two into the same setting on many occasions, and over a period of time. However, these latter organizations did not always foster the partners' interaction to the same extent. On some occasions, as we shall see, the two were merely encouraged to associate with each other. On other occasions, interaction was enforced; that is, the partners were constrained to see each other, as in the case of two of our subjects who had been required to work together as lab partners in a college biology course.

Let us turn to the Reluctants who met their partners through friends. It may seem odd, at first glance, that almost half of the Reluctants met their partners in this manner. Ordinarily, one assumes that friends will bring together only individuals they suspect will be warmly disposed to each other. However, if we look at our interview material more closely, it is apparent that these friends —some of whom were actually only "acquaintances"— certainly had not gone out of their way to engineer these meetings. Such introductions tended to be casual, unplanned, inadvertent. Not infrequently, while in the company of one of the partners, the "friend" just happened to bump into the other partner—at which time he introduced the two as a matter of course:

[JEWISH WIFE]: I met my husband in a restaurant. I was with my girl friend, who was going out with a friend of his. I was keeping her company while she waited. The two boys came along, and I was introduced to Frank. It wasn't planned—it just happened.

In contrast, several pairs of Amenables were introduced deliberately by friends who, undoubtedly, believed they would find each other congenial: ("Grace [a mutual friend] knew both of us well and gave each of us a big build-up to the other.") Since, supposedly, friends are selective in arranging such introductions and are not interested in bringing "uncongenials" together, we would expect that, as compared with Amenables, Reluctant couples (that is, where one or both of the partners was a Reluctant) would be united less frequently through the efforts of match-makers. If this is so—and for other reasons as well—we would expect Reluctants to meet their future partners more frequently in some kind of organizational setting. This hypothesis was borne out by our data.*

We shall presently trace some of the influences which led the Reluctant to date his partner after they had met.† But, first, it would seem logical to inquire into the Reluctant's general attitude toward interdating. Despite his resistance to intermarriage, was he willing to date persons of different religion? Moreover, was he as willing to date members of the outgroup as he was to date members of his own group? These questions are relevant, because if ethnicity was of no importance at this point, no special efforts are required to explain why the Reluctant dated the cross-ethnic he had

---

* Needless to say, an adequate test of this hypothesis would require a larger group of subjects.

† For purposes of this study, we have assumed that when one person "dates" another, this indicates that he is at least casually interested in that person.

just met. This might simply have been a reflection of the fact that no distinction was drawn between Jews and Gentiles insofar as dating was concerned.

On the basis of the data we collected, we are led to believe—not surprisingly—that, with one exception, all of the Reluctants preferred to consort with members of their own ethnic group. While the majority very clearly drew away from members of the outgroup, interestingly, perhaps half a dozen seemed to have had only slight reservations about interdating. We might speculate as to why those who recoiled at the thought of intermarriage were not more averse to dating individuals they would not consider marrying. While we have little data bearing on this point, there are a few factors which are worth mentioning. First, when an individual is very young (as was true of one of our respondents who was sixteen when he met his future wife), interdating may not be looked upon as dangerous because marriage seems so far off. Second, even though one is of marriageable age, it does not follow that one is necessarily marriage oriented. For example, a Catholic widow, who was advanced in years, told us that "it had never entered [her] mind to marry again." Since marriage was such a remote possibility, there was nothing to worry about when she met her future husband. However, later on, she became "very worried . . . and broke down and cried when [she] told the priest [she] wanted to marry a Jew."

Again, interdating may not cause the Reluctant much anxiety, if his interest is confined to sex. "During this period, I wasn't interested in getting married," said a Jewish male, "just in having a good time. I really didn't care what the girl's religion happened to be." He went on to explain that Christian girls were, in fact, preferable for his purposes: "Jewish girls are more moral, and it's harder to have a good time with them."

However, aside from this man (for whom, at this stage,

dating meant sex, not marriage),* on the whole, the Reluctants preferred to date those of similar background. In varying degrees, they were all disinclined to date those who were ethnically dissimilar.

Identification of the Partner's Ethnic Affiliation

Once the couple had met, what led the Reluctant to date, that is, to become even casually interested in an individual belonging to the outgroup? Why didn't the relationship come to a complete halt after the first meeting? Robert Merton's observation on the ways friendships form between those who hold disparate values would seem to have considerable bearing on this question:

In some proportion of cases, personal attachments will form in the course of repeated contact long before either partner to the relationship is aware that they are sharply at odds. . . . Once the relationship has become firmly established—which means only that the partners have experienced separate and mutual gratifications from their repeated interaction—it can, in some instances, tolerate a larger load of disagreement over certain values than is possible during the early phases, when the rela-

---

* One of the Jewish Amenable men we interviewed sought out Christian sex partners, not only because he believed they were more accessible sexually, but out of a fear of being trapped into marriage. If the girl was not Jewish, he reasoned that others (including the girl herself) would put less pressure on him to marry her. As he put it, "There was a certain safety in knowing she was of a different religion."

Speaking more generally, the same expectations will perhaps lead any males of this description—i.e., those who are wary of marriage, but looking for a sexual liaison—to seek out maritally "inappropriate" women. Such men may gravitate, for example, toward women who are older than they are, of a lower social level, or toward women who had been married previously. Ironically, in the course of a sexual relationship, the marriage-shy male may become genuinely attached to his sex partner, and, consequently, attached to someone he had formerly considered an unsuitable marriage partner.

tionship is fragile. The very same kind of disagreement would threaten or disrupt a developing friendship in its early stages.[1]

With reference to the Reluctants in our group, we might ask: At what stage in the relationship did they learn of their partners' deviant religious affiliation? Were any of them unaware of it initially and drawn to the other before they learned the "unpleasant news"? If so, did this make the revelation less threatening when it finally did come than would otherwise have been the case? Since these questions derive from the passage quoted above, which, unfortunately, came to our attention only after we had concluded the interviewing, our queries were not oriented toward eliciting such information. Nevertheless, some of our material is relevant in this connection. In the following passages we shall examine these data.

All of the interviewees were asked when they had learned of their partners' ethnic affiliation. We found that, as a group, the Reluctants were not long ignorant of the facts; the majority were aware of their partners' religion by the end of the first encounter. However, in three cases this information came to light at a later stage: in one case, during the second encounter; in another, after about six meetings. Finally, a Catholic woman (whose husband had a decidedly non-Jewish name and a "typical blonde, German look") didn't learn he was Jewish until they had become "very serious." Prior to the point of discovery in these three instances, there were no obstacles (at least no ethnic obstacles) to block the development of the Reluctant's feelings for his partner.

But what about the future? Did the fact that the Reluctant had felt some warmth for his partner before he learned the unpleasant news make the revelation less damaging to the relationship than it might have been otherwise? In the following passage, we can sense that the subject's early affection for her husband probably helped her to sustain the shock of finding out that he was Jewish:

[CATHOLIC WIFE]: We met for the first time when I walked into his store and started talking to him. I don't make friends easily, especially men. But I went into that store every night to buy things because he was open later than the other stores, and we talked together every night. . . . He was such a gentleman. I liked to speak with him in his store, and that's how I got to know him. . . . No, I didn't know he was Jewish from the beginning. I don't remember when I found out, but it must have been when he told me his name and I said, "Oh, are you of Spanish descent?" He said, "No, Jewish. Does that make any difference?" And I said, "No." I remember that when he told me he was Jewish, I couldn't believe it.

In another case in this group, a Catholic woman met her future husband in a company cafeteria, assumed he was a Christian, and was very favorably impressed. "I thought now there's a man with brains. He didn't go on with the usual silly office chatter." She then went on to describe an incident which occurred on their first date:

I got out of work and went to meet him. I had just blown up at my boss' assistant, who was a Jewish man. The first thing I said to John was how I hated that dirty kike, and that the one good thing Hitler did was to kill all those Jews. Later on in the evening he asked me what religion I thought he was. I said, "Episcopalian?" He said, "No, Jewish." Was I mortified!

In view of her anti-Semitism (which was apparent throughout the interview), she probably would not have dated her husband initially if she had been aware of his ethnic affiliation. Pursuing the matter further, we might speculate as to whether her favorable impression of him did not cushion the news of his being Jewish and make it more likely that she would see him again in the future. When asked why she had accepted a request for another date, she replied, "I thought I had to accept, so that he wouldn't think I was discriminating against *him*." From this we can infer that if he had been a total stranger when these anti-Semitic remarks were made, she would probably have felt less remorseful and been less determined to make amends.

Even when the Reluctant learned of the other's identity at the first meeting, timing may have made a difference (i.e., whether the identification was made at the beginning or end of the encounter). Thus, we might wonder whether one of our Jewish Reluctants, who struck up a conversation with his future wife at a skating rink, would have pursued the matter had he known she were Catholic right from the start:

I was not sure at first whether or not she was Jewish, but I found out before the evening was over. I learned what her name was when I took her home, and then I knew she was Italian. . . . My initial reaction was that I was taken aback. I had assumed she was Jewish, and when I heard she wasn't, there was a slight distaste. I was a little disappointed. I knew that my parents would not approve. I did not care to tackle all that if it wasn't necessary.

It is interesting to note some of the ways in which the Amenables differed from the Reluctants in this connection. In the first place, the Amenable had more difficulty in re-calling the precise point at which he had learned of his partner's religious affiliation: ("I just have no idea when I realized he was Jewish.") Secondly, a larger proportion of the Amenables learned of it at a later stage. Finally, when those who were initially ignorant did become informed of this fact, they were comparatively unconcerned; it was not a "shocking thing."

[PROTESTANT WIFE]: I found out he was Jewish two or three months after I met him. . . . I don't remember how it came up, but we were pretty serious about each other then. I don't think it made much impression on me; I had been going out almost exclusively with Jewish men at that time.

[PROTESTANT WIFE]: I think I wondered whether or not he was Jewish, but I was just speculating. It didn't make any difference. We were engaged before he told me anything about his background.

[JEWISH HUSBAND]: I don't recall just when I learned that she was non-Jewish. It was somewhere along the line. It must have come up in a discussion of some type. The whole thing just did not mean a great deal to me.

Thus, it did not make much difference *when* the Amenables quoted above learned of their partners' affiliation. Nor can it be argued, in sharp contrast to the Reluctants, that their initial non-awareness played any particular role in promoting their relationships.

Since a delay in recognizing their partners' ethnic affiliation apparently encouraged several of our Reluctants to outmarry, it becomes pertinent to consider the conditions under which Reluctants in the wider population are apt to make an incorrect identification initially. We can deal with this question by examining the ways in which our own particular subjects (both Reluctants and Amenables) became apprised of their partners' ethnic identity. We would assume that when Reluctants in the wider population are not able to utilize these sources, or when the information provided by them is obscure or misleading, they will be more apt to form an erroneous impression.

We have categorized in Table 6 the ways in which the persons we interviewed learned that their partners were Jewish or Gentile.

The largest number of respondents inferred their partners' ethnicity from his name or appearance. For the most

Table 6. Ways in Which Respondents Established Their Partners' Ethnicity

Inferred from partner's name or appearance	60%
Inferred from knowledge of partner's social milieu	33
Informed about it	25
	118%*
Number of respondents	(60)

* The percentages total more than 100 because some respondents derived their information from more than one source.

part, they felt that further confirmation was unnecessary: ("I knew he was a Christian from the beginning because of his name. It wasn't hard to guess." "I knew right away he was Gentile because of his first name—Jim. No Jewish boy ever had that for a name!" "After we talked a bit, it turned out we had been to the same high school. When I got home, I looked her up in the yearbook, and I noticed that her name sounded Jewish.")

Some interviewees had depended on appearance: ("I knew from the beginning he was Jewish because of his facial characteristics, and not because he said anything about it." "Did I know he was Jewish? Yes, unmistakably! If you could see him, you'd know what a silly question that is!" "I knew he was Gentile from the beginning—he had red hair and freckles." "I knew right away she was Catholic— she wore a cross.")

Many of those who inferred the facts from a knowledge of their partners' social milieu were guided by the ethnic affiliation of their partners' friends. It was tacitly assumed that friends would be ethnically similar: ("I thought he was a Gentile because the friend he was with was Gentile." "I knew from the start he was Jewish. I guess I just assumed it, because he was a friend of Jane's and Jane was Jewish.") Other indicators were the neighborhood or community in which the partner resided; the organizations with which he was affiliated (churches, colleges, businesses, and recreational groups); and his occupation: ("She was a nurse, and

Jewish girls from my background don't usually become nurses.")

On occasion, the information was conveyed verbally. Sometimes, the partner himself disclosed his identity, on his own initiative. A Jewish woman, apparently anxious to correct what she believed to be the mistaken notions of her suitor, recalled, "I felt I had misled him into thinking that I was Catholic, because I told him I had been to St. Patrick's for the Christmas Mass. . . . I remember telling him on our third date that I was Jewish." Sometimes the partner revealed his identity in response to the probings of the other:

[CATHOLIC HUSBAND]: At this lecture-dance where I met her, I was trying to guess her religion. I asked her if she was Scandinavian. She looks that type, you know, blonde. She said, "I'm Jewish."

[PROTESTANT WIFE]: One evening he said to me that nothing would come of this. I asked him why, and he said he would rather not say. I pressed him and finally asked him if it had anything to do with religion. He said that was it—that he was Jewish and his family wouldn't like it.

Finally, other people in the actor's milieu—relatives, friends, or acquaintances—occasionally made the facts known. In some instances, they did so in reply to the actor's direct queries. In other cases, they raised the issue on their own initiative: ("My roommate told me he was Jewish when he asked me for a date the first time." "There was someone at the university who made a point of telling me he was Jewish soon after we met—someone who thought we shouldn't have anything to do with each other.")

To return to the Reluctant as a general type, we can take it for granted that he will be anxious to establish the ethnic affiliation of the person he is currently dating or might date in the future. We can also assume that he will be sensitive to the kinds of cues that are typically employed. In this connection, Allport and Kramer observe: "The question of racial identity is of small importance to the person free from prejudice. Yet it is of considerable importance to the bigot, and for this reason the bigot apparently learns to observe and interpret both facial features and expressive behavior so that he can more swiftly spot his 'enemy.'"[2]

However, the Reluctant's ability to make a correct identification will still depend, in some measure, on certain specific characteristics of the situation, namely, the extent to which the indicators noted above are both present and reliable. We would expect that the Reluctant would be more likely to fail to identify his partner from the start under the following conditions: If the partner's name or appearance were "ambiguous" or misleading; if his knowledge of the partner's social milieu did not provide a ready basis for such inferences or if the available facts encouraged him to draw incorrect inferences; and if other people in the Reluctant's milieu knew nothing about the partner.

It was suggested previously that the fact that the Reluctant was unaware of his partner's true identity may have helped to account for his interest, i.e., for the fact that he dated such an individual. A few additional comments, which grow out of the preceding discussion, are in order at this point.

Quite apart from whether he acquires such information immediately or at some later date, once the Reluctant learns of his partner's affiliation, he has yet to discover how committed the partner is to his heritage. The knowledge that an individual is Jewish or Christian tells us nothing about the strength of his religious convictions (or, more generally speaking, his cultural ties). It may turn out that the partner is ardently committed to his religion—that he is a doctrinaire in his beliefs and zealous in his practices. On the other hand, he may be quite detached or even alienated from his religious-cultural background. Of course, these questions may be of little import to certain Reluctants. If their resistance to intermarriage derives wholly from social considerations, their partners' religious outlook will be of small concern. The typical anti-Semite, for instance, cares little whether the object of his contempt has ever set foot within a synagogue. On the other hand, the strength of the cross-ethnic's religious convictions may make a good deal of difference. In such cases if the partner is indifferent to his background, the romance, presumably, will be deterred to a lesser degree.

The questions which were raised earlier with respect to the point at which the Reluctant learned of his partner's ethnic affiliation might well be raised again in this context. That is, at what stage in the relationship did the Reluctant learn of his partner's religious outlook? What led him to become apprised of it? Finally, did the stage at which he became so informed affect the progress of the affair? While the data available do not enable us to answer these questions, a few comments bearing upon them are in order.

When we turn to the religious orientation of the Reluctants' partners (and we shall do so in greater detail later on), we find that, generally speaking, they were not strongly committed to their heritage. Typically, they were not fervent in their religious beliefs and practices, and one would suppose that, as a result, the Reluctants were less deterred from becoming involved. Accordingly, we would suggest that the *earlier* the Reluctants became acquainted with their partners' relative indifference to their religion (after having learned of their affiliation), the more likely it was that a close relationship would develop. Lack of data prevents us from exploring this process with respect to the Reluctants. However, the process itself can be roughly illustrated by the remarks of one of our Amenables:

[PROTESTANT HUSBAND]: No, I didn't feel at all hesitant about becoming involved with a Jewish person. Not at all, at least I do not remember any such feelings. . . . It only bothered me from the point of view of the children, and this came up early. When I became acquainted with her views, I realized there wouldn't be any problems.

While, in general, the partners of the Reluctants were relatively indifferent to their faith, in at least several instances they were ardently religious. In such cases, we would suggest that the *later* this fact became evident to the Reluctant, the more likely was the romance to continue (and for reasons similar to those previously noted). While, once again, we are unable to examine this hypothesis, the remarks of one of our Amenables may serve to illustrate the process we have in mind:

[CATHOLIC WIFE]: I didn't think of Irving as Jewish [at first]. To me, he didn't represent the Jewish religion or culture at all by the way he acted. . . . There was nothing about him that reminded me he was different until we started to get serious and got on the subject of religion.

4 . . . The Compensating

Aspects of the Partner

WITH A FEW EXCEPTIONS, the Reluctants in our group accurately identified their partners' ethnic status immediately. How is one to account then for the fact that they became "interested," at least interested enough to date them? Why didn't the relationship simply come to a halt after the Reluctant learned that his partner had the "wrong" affiliation?

Initial Hypotheses and Their Elaboration

Even before we began to interview our respondents, we were well aware, of course, that the ethnic affiliation of their mates would not be the only thing that had mattered to our group of Reluctants. Undoubtedly, like other marriage-oriented individuals, they had been hopeful of finding a partner who was a composite of many things— someone who possessed specific qualities, who responded to them in a particular way, who satisfied certain psychic needs. Accordingly, we surmised that perhaps their partners had been perceived as especially appealing in certain ways and that these positive qualities had offset the "obnoxiousness" of their ethnicity.

Clearly, this is not an unfamiliar interpretation of how such relationships may develop. To illustrate, if a young man who consistently dates only ravishing beauties becomes involved with someone who is extremely plain, in all probability, he considers her very outstanding in other ways. Compensation hypotheses of one type or another have frequently been advanced in the literature. For instance, in trying to explain interracial and interethnic marriages, the hypothesis has been entertained—and sometimes examined—that the minority member's socioeconomic position will be relatively high and that this will serve to offset his lower prestige.[1] Again, in reference to intercaste marriages, it has been suggested that the lower-caste female will be very attractive physically and that this pulchritude will offset her other deficiencies.[2]

We might add, at this point, that we made a special effort to explore the socioeconomic hypothesis above, as it applied to our own study. Thus, we compared the Reluctant's socioeconomic status with that of his partner at the time they met, and the partner's status with that of other individuals the Reluctant had dated. We wished to ascertain whether any discrepancies existed, and whether these might have accounted, at least in part, for the Reluctant's interest in his partner. However, as it turned out, there were very few discrepancies. When there was a disparity—and the Reluctant married an individual who belonged to a higher socioeconomic level—the difference was small, and there was little evidence to suggest that this was a significant factor. Despite a difference in emphasis, the following remarks by an Amenable Protestant woman are illustrative of the type of comments we thought the Reluctants might make. However, these expectations were not borne out.

What I liked most about my husband, compared with these other men I was going with, was his interests. He was interested in better things than they were. I mean, there's nothing wrong with ball games, but that was *all* they ever talked about. My husband was interested in philosophy and lots of other things. Most of these others were in a trade, like being a machinist or something. I knew if I married them I'd be a housewife, have children, and that would be all there'd be in my life. We would never grow or do anything different. Here there was a possibility for something else. I thought that with Stephen my life would be changing and growing all the time. For example, one boy I went steady with—his attitude toward my piano-playing was, "Well," he said, "after we're married you're not going to do that any more!" He thought it was all kind of silly.

To describe our thinking at the pre-interview stage of our study in greater detail, we entertained the notion that not only would the partner possess certain features sought after by the Reluctant, but that he would possess them to a greater extent than had the Reluctant's previous ingroup dating partners. If this were so, it might well account for the Reluctant's emerging interest. In formulating the questions for our interviews, we were guided by these conceptions; moreover, we hoped to obtain information that was comprehensive enough to allow us to investigate them in some detail. More specifically, at this preliminary stage of our research, we hoped to find out what type of person the Reluctant had wanted to marry; the degree to which his former ingroup partners fulfilled his requirements, as compared to his mate; his first impression of his mate-to-be; the factors which had led him to become interested in his future spouse; and those which determined his more serious involvement.

However, as the interviewing got under way, it became evident we would not be able to examine all of these questions, except in the most cursory manner. Given the limited amount of time at our disposal (a result of our earlier decision to explore a wide range of influences), we simply could not afford to linger very long on any given topic, no matter what the particular subject. As a result, some of the questions we had planned to investigate were dropped (e.g., the type of person the Reluctant had hoped to marry), and others were "lumped together."

The decision to eliminate certain questions and to combine others did not resolve our difficulties. Some of the topics dealt with in the interview were troublesome for the respondents; however, the most troublesome was our request that the subjects try to recall some of the things about their partners that had especially appealed to them. Not infrequently, the interviewee appeared to be at a complete loss, and the answers he finally supplied, even after lengthy consideration, were apt to be superficial: ("He had a nice personality." "We had common interests." "We just got along so well.") Generally, when we asked follow-up questions, it was possible to get him to elaborate on his answer and to specify what it was about his partner's personality that he thought was "nice." But this turned out to be a very arduous task for many of our subjects, and on some occasions they were simply unable to be more specific: °

There was nothing in particular about him that led me to become serious. I never thought about it that way, and I can't think now what there was. I just felt it. I'm more emotional than intellectual.

I don't know even now why there was such a congeniality or comfortableness between myself and Ruth. I can't put it in specific words even now.

° In their interviews with engaged couples, Ernest W. Burgess and Paul Wallin report that the partners were "seldom able to state why they fell in love with each other."[3]

Just why this question should have posed such difficulties
for our interviewees is an interesting topic in itself. Undoubtedly, part of the problem stemmed from the fact that
they were asked to recall earlier feelings and reactions. As
one young lady remarked, "I don't know how my husband
differed from other men I knew at the time. You know, you
become *prejudiced* about someone after you marry him."
Again, perhaps their difficulty derived from the fact that
they had never explicitly addressed themselves to the topic
before. Just as a person may never ask himself what it was
that led him to become an engineer, or a broker, or a sales-
man, so men and women who have fallen in love may never
examine thoroughly the basis of their attraction.* If this
question has not been grappled with previously, it may
prove troublesome when it is raised for the first time in an
interview situation. Finally, even though an individual may
be able to recall just what had appealed to him about his
partner, so many subtle factors may have been involved
that, when asked to recount them, he may simply be over-
whelmed by the magnitude of the task. Rather than coping
with such a complex issue in a relatively brief period of
time, the interviewee may decide that it would be less tax-
ing to slough off the question by declaring it unanswerable.

Whatever the reasons, we encountered a good deal of
difficulty in trying to ascertain the qualities the Reluctants
had found especially appealing in their partners. Very
likely, with more time at our disposal, certain of the obstacles noted might have been overcome. However, the
fact remains that, in general, the material we did manage
to collect on this phase of the investigation was incomplete
and shallow.

Despite these inadequacies, our original objectives re-

* In an investigation as to why young persons had chosen to pursue
certain occupations, the authors remark, "One of the interesting findings
that emerged from our interviews was that much of the material in [their]
decision-making was never before brought to the surface and discussed.4

mained essentially unaltered at the conclusion of the interviewing. In analyzing our material, we planned to let the Reluctant point out, so to speak, the specific features in his mate which had especially attracted him; and, if data were available, to compare his mate in these respects with individuals he had dated previously of his own ethnic group. This type of presentation would bring out the "strong points" of the partner, such as the fact that he was more gentlemanly than previous boy friends, or more intelligent, or more ambitious, or more worldly. However, the content of the interviews themselves raised certain questions which we had not considered originally. Ultimately, these questions led us to deviate from our earlier objectives and to embark on a somewhat different path. In order to explain the reasons for this departure and to outline the nature of certain hypotheses we developed subsequently, we shall retrace some of our thinking during the early phases of the analysis of our data.

With respect to the Reluctant's initial reaction to his partner, we found that the large majority were favorably impressed by the other and that a dating relationship was initiated not long afterward. Despite the partner's "obnoxious" ethnic affiliation, the Reluctant was very definitely impressed by certain other factors—at least to the point where he was willing to date. Since these findings were quite in harmony with our previous thinking, they raised few, if any, questions.

However, in half a dozen instances the Reluctant's initial reaction was either "lukewarm," or he was actually repelled by the other; in these cases, quite a period of time elapsed before a dating relationship developed. When we were confronted with these findings, our first reaction was to regard them as exceptions. We reasoned that, although the mate-to-be had never been considered markedly more attractive in certain ways than dating partners from the ingroup, perhaps the Reluctant's eventual interest in his partner could be explained adequately by other factors: Did he, for example, suspect that his partner's ethnicity would not constitute an insurmountable barrier and that his own affiliation would prevail in the event of a marriage? Were his friends extremely enthusiastic about the match? The evidence contained in the Reluctants' histories was inconclusive in this connection: We were neither compelled to accept, nor forced to reject, the idea that their courtships could be attributed to such "outside" factors.

At a later point we entertained the notion that these cases might not constitute exceptions after all. That is, these six Reluctants may have felt that their partners *were* much more desirable than members of the ingroup in certain important ways. But if this were so, how could we account for their initial lack of enthusiasm? The possibility then occurred to us that the Reluctant might not have perceived initially those attributes, qualities, traits, etc., which, at a later point, were to draw him to his future mate. To go a step further, perhaps the Reluctant's failure to recognize immediately his partner's strong points, rather than being due to any "blindness" on his part, was due to the fact that he was drawn by characteristics which, typically, one does not discern at a first meeting.

Before proceeding, let us formalize our thinking a bit with regard to these points. Obviously, when one person (A) first encounters another (B), much about the latter will represent an unknown quantity. Many of his attributes, qualities, traits, attitudes, values, etc., will be hidden from view initially. No matter how much A would like to penetrate B's opaqueness, to cast him under a fluoroscope which would reveal his inner depths, such wishes are bound to be frustrated at this point (assuming, of course, that A has no other sources of information regarding B). Only as A and B continue to interact, do B's initially hidden qualities emerge into view. All of this, of course, is merely by way of saying that one individual cannot really get to know another individual instantaneously. In essence, getting to know another person is a process of discovery—a process in which one becomes increasingly familiar with the inner layers of the other's personality and character.

Granted that, for the most part, a person's characteristics are not evident at a first meeting but only come to light in the course of time, the further question arises as to whether some features may not be more apparent than others. When individuals meet for the first time, do they typically become aware of certain characteristics before they become aware of others? Presumably, they do. To take a case in point, when young people were asked what characteristics they most desired in their future mates, they designated the following as being of primary importance: economic status, social class, education, age, and appearance; also stability and dependability, health, a desire for home life and children, and premarital sex experience.[5] We would suppose that the first group—starting with economic status and ending with appearance—would become known relatively early. (The high visibility of economic status, in addition to its intrinsic importance, is another reason it might be expected to act as a compensating factor in interethnic and interracial marriages.)

As for the other set of characteristics, we would assume that they would be relatively obscured from view initially. For example, the partner's stability and dependability (variously defined as sincerity, honesty, reliability, responsibility, steadiness, etc.)* will not be subject to immediate inspection. For the most part, insight into these characteristics is gained only in the course of observing the other's behavior over a period of time.

* These were regarded as the most important characteristics in Harold T. Christensen's investigation.[6]

Finally, we do not wish to imply that the characteristics of individuals with whom one comes into contact will emerge in a particular fixed sequence. It is somewhat grotesque to imagine that hundreds of young men, upon meeting members of the opposite sex for the first time, would become apprised of their social statuses on the first date, their temperamental qualities on the second date, their life goals on the third, etc. Clearly there are a score of other influences at work that will affect what A "sees" in B at any particular moment. For example, if A is anxious to learn some particular thing about B, he will learn about it more rapidly, as was the case with the Reluctants who quickly identified their partners' ethnic affiliation. Again, certain situations may act to unveil B's features more rapidly than will others. Thus, a crisis situation will bring certain of the interactors' qualities to the forefront more rapidly than will a routine date.* Again, B may purposely go out of his way to reveal certain of his characteristics or behave so as to enable A to infer their presence.† Despite the relevance of such processes, for purposes of the following discussion, we shall assume that they were nonoperative and that the stage at which an individual's character-

---

* One sociologist has suggested that it might be a good thing if young people sought out crisis situations. "There is a great danger that the conventional courtship masks, which hide distinctive characteristics of temperament, may extend through the engagement period and thus make impossible any attempt at evaluation of differences. One way to avoid this is to engage in activities which involve frequent crises of one kind or another, for anyone who is confronted by a crisis is thrown off his usual, habitual ways of reacting and tends to expose his basic traits."[7]

† Of course, B may also intentionally lead A to surmise things about him that are not true. In a more general sense, a problematic relationship exists between the image a person projects of himself and the person who is projecting the image. In the current study, however, these two levels of reality have been merged and treated as one—partly because pertinent data are lacking and partly because our interest centers on highlighting other dimensions of the partners' interaction. Nevertheless, in future studies of courtship we would certainly want to know more about the ways in which individuals endeavor to present themselves to others and the consequences this has for their affairs.[8]

istics become discernible will be wholly dependent upon their inherent observability.*

Turning to our empirical data in the light of the foregoing, we found some evidence to the effect that those Reluctants who had been unimpressed initially were later attracted to their partners by characteristics which an outsider would regard as being initially nonobservable. This led us to wonder how the Reluctants ever happened to become aware of their partners' redeeming features. Why hadn't they drawn away permanently, in view of their early indifferent or negative reaction? Significantly, it turned out that five out of six of these Reluctants were either encouraged or compelled by institutional forces to see their partners in the future. The institutional setting, it appeared, was at least partially responsible for bring to light the latent assets of their future mates.

Inevitably, the scheme we formulated led us to have certain expectations with regard to the other set of Reluctants in our group, i.e., those who had been favorably impressed initially. We suspected—and our suspicions were con-

---

* The distinction between visible and invisible characteristics may throw some light on why certain ethnic group stereotypes which are essentially untrue may be more durable than others. When the negative traits imputed to a group are nonobservable—e.g., when the members of that group are said to be "deceitful," "out for themselves," "oversexed"— they may be less subject to question and therefore more difficult to eradicate. Others having casual contact with group members may not be led to question the existence of these traits—just because such contact is merely casual. On the other hand, if the traits imputed to a group are of a visible nature, their authenticity may be questioned even though contact is of a casual nature. This is illustrated by the comments of a white housewife, living in an interracial housing project: "I thought I was moving into the heart of Africa. I had always heard things about how they were . . . they were dirty, drank a lot . . . were like savages. Living with them, my ideas have changed altogether. They're just people. They're not any different."⁹

However, as contact increases between members of privileged and underprivileged groups and as ethnic stereotypes come to be questioned, there may be a tendency to impute negative traits of a more invisible kind. For example, instead of being viewed as "dirty," the minority member may be viewed as "untrustworthy."

firmed to some degree—that in these instances certain of the important assets possessed by the partner were of a highly visible nature and that these were largely responsible for immediately activating the Reluctants' interest.*

To review the transition in our thinking, at the conclusion of the interviewing, we had merely planned to call attention to the various appealing and/or differentiating features of the partner that were primarily responsible for activating the Reluctant's interest. At this point, we had no thought of conceptualizing these characteristics in terms of their visibility. However, when we found that certain of the Reluctants had not been at all enthusiastic about their partners at the start, we began to wonder whether the partners in these instances actually lacked important compensatory features or whether the attraction of both those Reluctants who were favorably impressed initially and those who were not might still be accounted for satisfactorily by some theory of compensating characteristics. In trying to resolve this problem, we were led to conceptualize characteristics—whether they happened to be social statuses, personality traits, or whatever—in terms of their observability and to formulate the following hypotheses: The Reluctants who had been favorably impressed initially became interested in their future spouses because the latter possessed certain differentiating features of a highly visible kind. The Reluctants who had been unimpressed became attracted to their partners later, because their partners possessed—and they eventually discerned—certain differentiating features of an initially invisible kind; moreover, the institutional setting in which these couples found them-

* It should be pointed out that our post-interview thinking did not proceed in the compartmentalized fashion we have suggested. Solely in an effort to make our exposition clear, we have implied that the hypotheses were formulated without any reference to the interview material at our disposal, and that these ideas were then examined in the light of the available data. Actually, to a great extent, the interview material itself prompted the ideas outlined.

selves played an important role in bringing these latent assets into view.*

In the following passages we shall examine our data in the light of these hypotheses. However, because these hypotheses were formulated at the conclusion of the interviewing and extensive data are therefore lacking, our interpretive comments can only be considered suggestive. With these limitations in mind, we shall first examine some of the Reluctants who were favorably impressed with their partners from the start and then turn to the six Reluctants who were initially unenthusiastic about their future mates.

The Partner's Characteristics and Their "Observability"

RELUCTANTS WHO WERE FAVORABLY IMPRESSED INITIALLY

A Catholic husband told us how he happened to become interested in his mate:

She was no spender, and she wasn't just looking for a good time. She treated me nice. She wasn't a loud girl. I had respect for her and she had respect for me. [*How did she differ from other girls you knew?*] *She could converse with me, she could keep up a conversation.* [*Could she converse better than other girls you knew?*] She was better than the others I knew. *I really admired her for that.*

Among other features, this man emphasized the fact that his wife could keep a conversation going. How important was it for him to find such a mate? From his history, we

* The reader will recognize that we are not the first to make use of observability (or visibility) as a concept in social science. Robert Merton has indicated that the concept was first obliquely introduced by Simmel, and that a good deal of current research is concerned with matters bordering upon it. After pointing out that observability can profitably be looked upon as constituting a property of groups, Merton considers at length certain of the linkages between this property and organizational theory.[10]

note that he came to this country from Italy at the age of seven and that he had only dated a few times before he met his wife; moreover, he was repeatedly described by his wife as having been "terribly shy." We are thus led to believe that he was probably very ill-at-ease on a date and that his wife's fluency was of importance precisely because it reduced his feeling of awkwardness. Furthermore, we would regard conversational proficiency as a feature which is readily observable. Undoubtedly, our subject learned right away of his partner's skill and for this reason, among others, was immediately attracted to her.

Turning to another instance, a Protestant woman—whose family was socially prominent—described how she happened to become interested in her Jewish husband (the son of Orthodox Jews who had emigrated from Eastern Europe):

I was getting fed up with the men I was going with. There was a lot of heavy drinking in the crowd, and if there was no cocktail party to go to, they were at a complete loss as to what to do. . . . My husband differed from these other men because he had *no sophistication*. He never knew what was the right thing to do or say. And his speech was so terribly different from theirs. When we were with my friends and he would say "tomato" and my friends would say "tomahto," there would be a dreadful silence. Then, all the things which had been part of my life, like sailing and tennis and the rest of it, Arthur had never had. He knew no sports and had worked his way through college. Money meant something to him. I had simply thrown it away, and I couldn't understand at first why he didn't want to spend money going to night clubs every night. . . . He had never had the little niceties that we took for granted—birthday parties and that sort of thing—*things I was able to give him and felt I wanted to very much.*

It is evident that her husband's lack of "sophistication," his "spartan" background, and his unfamiliarity with her style of life had set him off sharply from other men of her acquaintance. Had she been hopeful of finding someone of this description? Aside from her remarks above, to the effect that she relished providing him with the "little niceties" of life, at another point she disclosed she had hoped to find someone who "would lean on her." Finally, we would regard one's "worldliness" or lack of worldliness as an observable feature, a feature that generally does not escape the notice of others and which did not go unrecognized for long by this particular subject.

In passing, the remarks made by this woman's husband about his background and why "proper form" came to hold such appeal for him are worth noting. They are of interest because they reveal how well the requirements of the two partners dovetailed.

Before I met my wife, I never thought much about mixed marriages, but I guess I had the feelings in my bones that I probably would not marry a Jewish girl. . . . Looking back, I may have been trying to avoid Jewish girls. There was just something about them that I did not like—it was probably a kind of subconscious feeling I had. [*What didn't you like about them?*] It's hard to say. The ones I met were not brought up with a proper sense of values—they were overmaterialistic, I just didn't think they behaved properly, they didn't have any manners. Frankly, I was embarrassed when I was in their company.*

How did I feel about being Jewish when I was growing up? I just thought that being Jewish was what everybody was. I thought the non-Jews were an exception—this was because I lived in a Jewish neighborhood and had little contact with the

---

* This respondent was not alone in his dim view of the Jewish female. Interestingly, over half a dozen of our subjects pictured the typical Jewess as spoiled and demanding: ("Jewish girls have the attitude: 'Here I am, *do* for me! Buy me a Cadillac and a mink coat'." "Jewish girls *want*— Gentile girls don't demand so much." "Jewish wives start complaining the minute they're pregnant and sit home all day. . . . As soon as the baby is born, they start playing mahjong all the time, instead of keeping a clean home and cooking good meals for their husbands.")

outside world. . . . No, I didn't feel that being born Jewish was a burden when I was growing up. It was only when I started college; then I felt that way all the time. . . . At Princeton, I discovered I didn't know the ways of the world. When I started there, I realized how narrow my existence had been. The only things that I had known were the ways of my mother. To give you an instance of how different these worlds were—if someone did something nasty, my mother would say, 'What do you expect, he's not Jewish!' [*What was unfamiliar about this world to you?*] The boys at Princeton just had a different upbringing. . . . Their ways of meeting people and their ways of acting in public were foreign to me; it was nearly a different culture. Because of their social background they had a certain flexibility about them. Such things were strange to me. . . .

As far as understanding my background, I think the year that I spent in Spain was very important, as was also my entering this new world at Princeton. [*The subject spent a year abroad as an exchange student.*] In Spain I lived with a noble family. . . . The experience made quite an impression upon me. I admired their life and loved it. [*What appealed to you about their way of life?*] It was an accumulation of small things, although it might be subsumed under a few general headings. There was the proper way that people invite you to their home, there was the attitude toward guests when they were in the home, there was the respect that parents and children showed for each other. These were just instances of some of the things that appealed to me. Their whole way of life was different—everything from sending you a thank-you note for a present to knowing when to rise when a lady came into the room. All this may seem terribly superficial to you and give you an awful sense of my values— but I do feel that proper form is important and it does make life more pleasant. . . . In view of my liking for this type of life and the setting of my life at Princeton—it was perfectly logical that I should marry my wife. My wife is at the top of the social ladder; her parents are among the elite."

In the following passages we shall present the comments of other Reluctants who indicated some of the important ways in which their mates differed from their ingroup dating partners. As was the case earlier, we would regard the differentiating characteristics singled out below as being inherently observable, that is, as features that as a rule are readily noticeable.

[JEWISH WIFE]: When he came to see me that night [after our first meeting], I was living by myself in a four-room apartment. . . . You shoulda seen how I was dressed—in a sweater and slacks. I dressed very unladylike so I wouldn't have any trouble with fellows who came to call. When he left he shook hands with me. It almost knocked me over he was *so polite.* . . . How did he differ from Jewish boys I knew? No difference, really. Well, he was *so polite,* and *older,* and never tried to start anything.

[JEWISH FIANCÉE—whose suitor came from South Dakota]: He made a favorable impression upon me, but I felt it was no use because we were worlds apart. This wasn't just a matter of religion, but our whole backgrounds. I decided this after I just knew the vital statistics about him. . . . He was different from other boys I knew because *he had a refreshing personality which was not the brash smart-aleckiness of others I knew.* There was no suggestiveness in the way he acted. . . . He was corney in a charming sort of way.

[JEWISH WIFE]: While I was going out with Larry, I wasn't serious about any other men, but I knew some others [they were all Jewish]. The outstanding thing about Larry was he always looked *clean.* Some people are like that. No matter what they wear, they always look clean and nice. He was different too— his background was different from ours [i.e., from members of her circle]. He hadn't had a father since he was a baby and his mother kept him down. He was *very much the gentleman* while the other seventeen year old boys I knew weren't—they were loud and boisterous. My parents always liked Larry. When my mother didn't know we were serious about each other or that we were going out together, she said, "If that boy were Jewish I'd love to have him for a son-in-law."

To further illustrate, a Jewish doctor—who was primarily interested in sex, who felt that Christian girls were "easier to have a good time with," and whose partner was a nurse—succinctly, but meaningfully, conveyed his first impression: "A nice gal, good looking, well stacked." In another instance, an eighteen-year-old Jewish girl, who had had little previous dating experience, was impressed by her partner's social poise: "George was the first grown-up I'd been out with. He was so sure of himself. He could order meals in a restaurant. He was good at talking to people. He always put me at my ease."

Let us take note of one final case which merits attention by virtue of the fact that the important differentiating characteristic might easily have gone unrecognized initially. When asked how his wife differed from other girls he knew, this Jewish husband replied:

The predominant way was that she was not a phony. The others were far too egocentric. They were far too wrapped up in themselves. *They were far too concerned about how their actions would appear to others. Their behavior was controlled by what others might think.* Their whole pattern of life was laid out for them. This was less true of my wife.

Apparently, he immediately visualized her as being an independent type of person—someone who was not subservient to convention, or cowed by the opinions of others. We say "immediately" because, aside from his being favorably impressed right from the start, he was one of the few Reluctants to fall in love very rapidly. "If the right two hands happen to touch, it is like an electric charge. That is exactly the way it was with us."

How did this man come to the conclusion so quickly that his mate-to-be was an "inner-directed" type? Certainly, it is easy to imagine a situation in which one would fail to recognize the presence of such qualities in the first few encounters. As it turned out, through a combination of circumstances, this wife's independence of mind was immediately revealed to her husband. He learned right away that she was legally separated from her husband, but that both had continued to live at her aunt's house, the only difference being that they now occupied separate rooms; furthermore, both looked upon this as comprising a permanent living arrangement. The wife commented on her husband's reactions to this unconventional domestic set-up: "Irving was fascinated by my situation—that Charlie and I were separated but still living in the same house." In brief, it would appear that a unique constellation of circumstances immediately gave this Reluctant a strong hint that his partner's behavior was "not controlled by what others might think."

As we mentioned previously, the Reluctants who were favorably impressed from the start generally began to date soon after the first meeting. At the same time, it should be noted that half a dozen of these subjects met their partners within institutional settings which served to bring the two partners into contact over a period of time. The fact that in these instances the Reluctant's response to his future partner was immediately affirmative does not mean that these external factors played no role in perpetuating the relationship. There is reason to believe they were of considerable importance. In fact, had such influences not been present, the marriage might not have occurred:

[CATHOLIC WIFE]: We worked together as class officers during our senior year. We got along very well and accomplished a great deal. We were both the kind who could compromise, so we got a lot done. I think this brought us closer together, because we found out what sort of people we were. [*Do you think anything would have happened if you'd been introduced by friends and hadn't worked together?*] I don't know whether we would have gotten interested. I think so, but I really couldn't say for sure.

[CATHOLIC WIFE]: We worked together in the same company, but not in the same office. Yes, it helped bring us closer together, because otherwise I wouldn't have seen him so much. [*Do you think anything would have happened if you'd been introduced by friends and hadn't worked together?*] I don't think we would have become interested in each other. I know we wouldn't. It would have been enough for me that he was Jewish to stop it.*

RELUCTANTS WHO WERE "LUKEWARM"
OR REPELLED INITIALLY

　　In view of their initially unfavorable impression, how did these six Reluctants happen to become interested in their partners later? Let us briefly repeat and elaborate the hypotheses outlined earlier. It was suggested that in these instances the partners were more appealing in certain ways than were ingroup marital prospects, but that the Reluctants were not immediately aware of those features which were to draw them to their partners. Their initial nonawareness, in our view, was due to the fact that their partners' strong points were of a type that are apt to escape immediate notice. The Reluctants began to date their partners, we suggested, only as they began to fathom what lay beneath the surface.

　　As to how they did eventually become apprised of their partners' strong points, we believe that the institutional setting in which five out of six of these couples found themselves was instrumental in bringing these features into view. Looking at these settings a bit more closely, we find that in two of the five instances, the partners—while they did not have to associate with each other—were encouraged to interact by the nature of the situation. (One of these couples was in the same section of a freshman class in

* It will be recognized that these and other "institutional" couples in our group can be readily placed within the framework developed by George Homans. More explicitly, the external system, by initially inducing the partners to interact, laid the foundation for the later emergence of an internal system.[11]

law school; another belonged to an army officer's social club whose members did a good deal of socializing.) Interaction between the partners was fostered in a variety of ways: The partners were in close proximity; because of their common interests, they had a ready-made basis for engaging in conversation; and they had or later developed mutual acquaintances who, in turn, encouraged them to see more of each other. In three of the five instances, whether they liked it or not, the partners were *constrained* to associate with each other by the organizational set-up. (In one instance, the partners were assigned to work together as lab partners in a college biology course; in another, they had worked side by side in a factory and their job activities were interdependent; and in a third, they were members of a small graduate seminar whose members met once a week for the entire day.) Overlooking the differences between these two sets of environmental conditions (those which encouraged the pair to interact versus those which constrained such interaction), we suggested that these institutional forces, by inducing the two to associate, played a significant role in bringing the partner's latent assets into view.

It will be recognized that we have put forward a number of discrete hypotheses, and that if they are to be adequately "tested" by the data, each of these requires answers to certain distinctive questions. However, for reasons previously indicated, it is not possible to carry out a conclusive "test." Instead, we shall merely try to demonstrate the plausibility of the ideas outlined. With this as our objective, we shall examine the six cases referred to above in greater detail.

The Reluctant in the first case, a Catholic fiancée who had been in the same section of a freshman law school class as her husband, remarked, "I never thought I'd fall in love with him. His looks and his manner didn't appeal to me." We then asked her why she had become drawn to him:

We understood each other. He's exactly like I am in many respects and for a good reason—we come from such similiar backgrounds, by which I mean our problems with our families are just alike. [*Both families, incidentally, were strongly opposed to the marriage.*] [*How did he differ from Gentile boys you knew?*] He's the most sensitive person . . . and he's more understanding. He's much brighter than any boy I'd ever known. . . . Also I was going with such a cad at the time that he was good in contrast.

It does not seem strange that certain of her fiance's differentiating characteristics (the fact that his problems with his parents were similar to hers, his "understanding" qualities, etc.) were not immediately apparent. Ordinarily, we would not expect such features to be observable at the start. From her remarks we can sense that the external setting helped to bring these appealing aspects into view:

[*How did you get to know each other?*] At law school, in classes together. We went to dances, parties, movies, ate together, studied together.

The second subject, a Protestant wife, briefly described the first meeting and her early feelings about her future husband:

We met first at a party. We were both with other people at a large group at an Officer's Club dance in Louisville. We happened to be at the same table. We didn't exchange two words at the time. It just happened that each of us knew everyone at the table but us. I remember all the people there were Protestant. Sidney was the only one I didn't like that evening.

In time, she became drawn to him because he "was more mature than other men she had known and was more the kind of man you want to marry." We do not know to what extent the Officer's Club was directly responsible for bringing his "mature" qualities into view. In any event, it undoubtedly played a vital role in initiating a dating relationship between the two:

My first impression was *unfavorable*. But we both went to the same club every weekend and saw each other there all the time. There were a lot of parties there, and we were part of a large group that was always together. Finally he asked me out. I guess I got over my unfavorable impression, because we saw a lot of each other at the club before I ever went out with him.

In another instance, a Jewish man and his future wife worked next to each other in a sweater factory, and their job activities were interdependent. Recalling his first impression, the man remarked, "I didn't like the way she dressed, I didn't like her religion, and I didn't like the way she talked." Because this Reluctant was extremely sensitive with regard to anything having to do with his courtship (he told us he only agreed to be interviewed out of deference to the rabbi who had given us his name), we could ask him only the most innocuous questions. When we ventured to ask why he had become attracted to his wife, he became so touchy and defensive that this line of questioning had to be abandoned.*

However, from his wife's comments, we would gather that the institutional setting played a significant role in overcoming his resistance and awakening his interest in her. His wife remarked, "I saw him at work, I saw him all day long. I remember the first time he kissed me—we were

---

* Throughout the study it will be noted that the wives are quoted more frequently than the husbands. In part, this was because there were twice as many female as male Reluctants. However, aside from this, as a group, the husbands seemed to be more ill-at-ease during the interview, and their responses were more apt to be abrupt or evasive. The wives, on the other hand, were more apt to express themselves freely and fully and apparently felt less constraint.

In a similar connection, in his study of Puerto Rican husbands and wives of the lower income group, Stycos notes that the men were more apt to be resistant when it came to answering "intimate" questions and that, generally speaking, they were less "articulate" throughout the entire interview.[12]

working overtime." Pointing to another environmental condition which, presumably, led the partners to see even more
of each other on the job than might otherwise have been
the case, she noted, "No, my husband and I didn't have any
friends in common. At work they were all Puerto Ricans,
and we didn't make friends with *them*."

In the fourth case, because their names happened to be
adjacent to each other in the alphabet, a Jewish Reluctant
and his partner were assigned as lab partners in a college
biology course. Once again, the Reluctant was not favorably
impressed by his partner at the start. When we asked him
what it was about his partner that eventually came to
appeal to him, his responses were not very revealing. We
could only find out that he felt his wife was smart; that
they had common interests—biology, sports, and reading;
and that his romance was "just one of those things that
evolve." The external setting may well have played a part
in activating his interest in the girl. At the very least, we
know the two were constantly thrown together: "Mostly
we got to know each other at first, because we were in two
classes together and we were also lab partners. This meant
we had the same lab section together, shared a desk, and
spent several afternoons a week working together."

In this case, there was an interesting sidelight—one
which had consequences for the affair. Here, the girl, not
the boy, took the first step in advancing the relationship—
by inviting him to a banquet given by a biological society.
Despite her friendly overtures, his lack of enthusiasm for
her continued. Not long afterward, however, he took the
initiative and asked her out on a date: "I felt obliged to ask
her out, since she had asked me. Then after that I started to
get serious." Since the fact that he reciprocated for her
invitation turned out to be a crucial turning point in the
affair, it is worth probing a bit further. Were his actions
prompted solely by courtesy, or were they also prompted
by the external setting to some extent? We would be in-

clined to believe that he felt constrained to ask her out because he realized that he and the girl were bound to see a good deal of each other in the future, and it would impose a strain upon their working relationship if he were to let his indifference be known. In other words, had he been invited out by a girl who was *not* his lab partner, presumably, he would have felt less obliged to return the favor—with the result that the relationship might not have progressed beyond the first date.*

The fifth case is, without question, the most illuminating for our purposes. Unlike the previous cases, it enables us to document, rather than merely allude to, certain processes which our hypotheses predicted. The following points clearly emerge: (a) The partner's appealing features—which led to his being preferred to candidates from the ingroup—were of an invisible kind; (b) the Reluctant's interest became activated only as he became aware of these features; (c) the external setting was instrumental in bringing these features into view:

[JEWISH WIFE]: In the first class I had at Rutgers he was there also, and there was a lot of discussion in the class. I was very talkative and he was very quiet and never said a word. My first impression was that he was quiet and confused—that is, he was mixed up personally. I felt he was preoccupied with his own worries and not paying much attention to what was going on around him. Then, about six months later, we were in this counseling class together, and we all got to know each other very well. This was a seminar that met once a week for the entire

* What occurred between these two people nicely illustrates certain observations recently made by Gouldner with reference to "starting mechanisms" and the "norm of reciprocity": "People are continually brought together in new juxtapositions and combinations, bringing with them the possibilities of new social systems. How are these possibilities realized? Is such realization entirely a random matter? . . . [The functionalist] may suspect that certain kinds of mechanisms, conducive to the crystallization of social systems out of ephemeral contacts, will in some measure be institutionalized or otherwise patterned in the society. At this point he would be considering 'starting mechanisms.' In this way, I suggest, the norm of reciprocity provides one among many starting mechanisms."[13]

day. We would interview clients and then discuss the interviews amongst ourselves. I began to feel that Harry was the only one I could share my impressions of the other people and my work with. But I never thought of going out with him, as I had decided I would never marry a non-Jew. But we happened to live nearby and we always went home together on the subway and talked. Then, we'd have lunch together sometimes, too. After a few months of this I decided his not being Jewish was really no barrier, and I would just accept what came of the relationship. . . .

Around Christmas was when he first asked me for a date. On our first date we discussed our families and religion and everything. He put his whole personality on the table, so to speak, and we talked in a way which showed that we were really pretty serious about each other, even though we'd never gone out before. . . .

Having the class together certainly brought us closer together. We hadn't paid any attention to each other before. It was because we found out that we could discuss so many things with each other. [*Suppose you had been introduced by friends and hadn't been in the class together?*] I don't know whether we would have gotten interested in each other. It all would have depended on how he acted. Usually, he acted very retiring when he first met people, and if he had been that way I wouldn't have been interested. Being in the class together, I got to know him and found that he had very original ideas and was very interesting and not at all retiring when he got to know people.

When asked to compare her husband with other young men known to her at the time, she continued:

They were all awful There was a super-conventional one, Jewish, getting his Ph.D. at Yale. Then there was a Jewish boy I met through my family. He was terribly tied to his mother's apron strings. Harry was more of an individual than any of them—the others were such stereotypes. Harry was much more interested in growing up and becoming more mature. He was more able to see reality. He was more ready to face life and not have so many illusions.

From her remarks, we can see that the kinds of characteristics which drew her to her husband (e.g., "original ideas,"
"able to see reality," "ready to face life," etc.), are not qualities that are usually discerned immediately. Had the couple
not been thrown together in an institutional setting, quite
possibly, these features would not have been revealed,
and the romance would not have developed.

An Amenable woman's description of her courtship will
be interjected at this point because she had been negatively
impressed initially and her remarks are suggestive of the
processes we have been discussing:

[CATHOLIC WIFE]: We met for the first time on the ward in the
hospital. I was a new nurse, and he was a resident in the ward.
We were introduced as a matter of course. I didn't like him at
first. I was frightened by his big burly look. He was not the
sort of man I'd imagined I would ever fall in love with. He was
too overpowering. . . .

We got to know each other after we met because we worked
together on the same ward for a month. We used to see each
other at intervals, when he would be assigned to the ward for a
day or two at a time. We didn't go out together for about two
or three months after we met. Then we used to go out once a
week at first, and we also made a point of meeting each other
at the hospital.

Working together brought us closer together. We were working intimately for the patients' welfare. It's a give and take
sort of relationship between nurse and physician—each is dependent upon the other. If we'd been introduced by friends and
hadn't worked together, I don't think I would have been interested in him. I was lukewarm about him at the beginning.

[*How did your husband differ from other men you had known
before?*] It's hard to say just how he differed. How can you
say why you fall in love? It's very difficult. . . . It happened so
slowly, or rather, insidiously. It just wasn't one thing that led
me to become serious about him, but it all happened over a
period of time. . . . While I was working with him, I had a high
regard for him and admiration. Seeing him with other people

at the hospital, I came to know what sort of person he was. I had never known other men as intimately. After all, a date is a made-up situation. You get all dolled up and put on your best manners. Working in the hospital with him, I got to know him very well, very fast.

From these remarks, we can hardly fail to conclude that the work situation was instrumental in disclosing just "what sort of person he was."*

To leave our own group of respondents for a moment, a great many studies have shown that the greater the contact (under certain conditions) between those who differ racially or ethnically, the more likely are mutually favorable attitudes to develop.[14] Moreover, in a study of interracial housing, referred to earlier, it was demonstrated that there is a correlation between the amount of prior contact and the likelihood of Negro-white friendships.[15] With regard to the relationship between these two variables, Homans writes, in more general terms: "The more frequently persons interact with one another, the stronger their sentiments of friendship for one another are apt to be."[16] However, the question arises as to *why* an increase in interaction should lead to an increase in friendliness. In other words, what are the intervening processes involved? As a preliminary measure, and in accord with the conceptions outlined earlier, it might be useful to think of this matter in

---

* However, even though institutional contact is responsible for the fact that two persons come to view each other as appealing, it may simultaneously erect obstacles to the further development of the relationship. Note the remarks of this woman's husband, who felt it would be embarrassing, under the circumstances, to be turned down by his future wife: "I was anxious to ask her for a date after I had found out about her background. . . . Ordinarily I did not date nurses. But she was different from other nurses. I noticed the way she spoke. Also the fellows . . . told me she was interested in modern dancing. This kind of intrigued me, because most of the nurses I knew were not like that—we viewed them just as a pushover for an easy lay. The whole thing intrigued me and I wanted to find out more about her. . . . On the other hand, I was afraid to ask her for a date. . . . *Being refused a date by her seemed kind of traumatic to me, because we saw each other all the time. It would be embarrassing.*"

the following way: As two persons continue to interact, their latent characteristics emerge into view; the augmented picture that each person now has of the other serves to draw them closer together.

Since such interaction is sometimes instituted by various organizational settings, the nature of the interaction so instituted might be differentiated in terms of how conducive it is (potentially speaking) to exposing the characteristics of each individual to the other. At one extreme, the contact instituted between the pair may be superficial in nature, confined to specialized areas, and occur only infrequently. At the other extreme, it may be profound, extensive in the areas covered, and occur with great frequency. It would seem that the closer the interaction pattern approximated the latter type, the more effective it would be in bringing the interactors' latent characteristics to the forefront.[17]

Of course, it does not follow that two persons who find themselves in a "high compression" setting and who, as a result, are thrown closely together will necessarily become drawn to each other. As they become aware of the other's latent characteristics, they may come to feel increasingly cool toward the other. However, if they were unfavorably impressed to begin with and were not constrained to interact, the chances are they would separate even before learning whether or not there was more to the other than "met the eye." In other words, the environmental setting may lead them to discover that they are actually congenial after all.

At this point, let us return to our data and examine the sixth instance in which the Reluctant's initial reaction was not enthusiastic. In this case, unlike the others, the couple were not brought together and drawn closer by an institutional setting. Rather, the wife, a Catholic—whose future husband had not looked "too keen" to her initially—became attracted to him solely in the course of dating. When we asked her why, in view of her first unfavorable impression,

she had seen him again, she replied: "He used to come to
the house a lot after I first met him, saying he had come
'to see my mother'." Significantly enough, because the
partner was a male—and so was able to take the initiative
—he was in a position to over-ride her resistance to seeing
him (although he went about it in a rather devious way).
If the situation had been reversed—i.e., if her husband had
been the one who was unimpressed initially—and external
influences promoting interaction were again lacking, it is
less likely that an attachment would have developed.*

Two other aspects of this case are worth noting. For one
thing, the two partners were members of the same clique—
the boy had joined her brother's "ice-cream crowd" of
which she was also a member. While in the Army, he had
become friendly with a member of the clique; after being
discharged, he renewed the friendship, was introduced to
her brother, and in this manner was drawn into the group.
The girl remarked, "We went out a lot with my brother
and his girl and the whole crowd of people that we knew
. . . we had all our friends in common." Perhaps informal
groups of this nature may serve the same function as the
more formal institutional settings considered above. By
encouraging two members to associate with each other,
they may unveil the hidden virtues of each. But we have
no way of knowing whether this was actually so in the case
at hand.

Although we will deal more fully with the question of
the partner's responsiveness at a later point, it is interesting
to note here that, in accounting for her husband's appeal
prior to their marriage, the wife emphasized—almost ex-

* This "prediction" is consistent with the findings of a study of 200
marriages in England: Whereas only 2 of the men were repelled on first
meeting their mates, 25 of the women were initially repelled.[18] The greater
initiative taken by the man in courtship may have other results as well.
The authors of another study suggest that it may account for their finding
that, both before and after marriage, women are more anxious to make
changes in their husbands than their husbands are to make changes in
them.[19]

clusively—his interest in her, rather than any objective characteristics he may have possessed:

My husband was different from the other fellows I knew because he was shy and nice and sweet. I became serious about him because he was so much nicer to me than the other fellows had been. He was respectful. I'd been going out with an Italian boy who was not very polite or nice. Herbie was a doll!

Evidently, her partner's responsiveness, coupled with the fact that her former boy friends had not been models of perfection, were primarily responsible for activating her interest in her future mate.

In the course of this chapter, we formulated a number of hypotheses (and examined our data in the light of these hypotheses) as to why the Reluctants in our group became interested in their partners. Whether the scheme we have outlined is actually useful in explaining how such relationships develop will, of course, depend on subsequent research findings in this area. However, at this point, the scheme at least provides a tentative approach to the subject at hand.

In order to summarize our thinking and bring to the forefront a few remaining questions with respect to the topic under consideration, we shall make use of a hypothetical situation. Let us suppose that one hundred Reluctant Jewish men will shortly meet Christian women, each of whom happens to embody more of the features these men consider desirable in their future mates than any of their ingroup dating partners. Furthermore, let us assume that half of these men are determined to find women with characteristics which we would label as "readily observable." They hope to find someone, for example, who is beautiful, sophisticated, wealthy, well-educated, articulate, witty, etc. On the other hand, we will suppose that the remaining fifty Jewish men are preoccupied with finding someone who has certain characteristics which would be regarded as typically nonobservable, e.g., someone who would be a good mother, someone who is sexually responsive, conscientious, resourceful, "well-adjusted," etc.* Assuming that each of the one hundred Jewish men recognizes immediately that the woman is Gentile, is there any basis for predicting which of these men might become romantically interested?

First of all, we would expect that most, if not all, of the members of the first group would be attracted to the women, because they would immediately discern that their partners were well endowed with the particular features they were seeking. Which of the members of the second group would be more likely to become interested? In accordance with the hypotheses developed above, it would be those men who became apprised of their partners' inner attributes, qualities, and traits. In this connection, we would want to know which, if any, of these couples would be encouraged (or forced) by external influences to interact in the future, because the external setting, by inducing them to associate, may bring to light characteristics which are initially hidden.

However, what about the remaining men in the second group, i.e., those who would not be induced by outside forces to see their partners again? Will they simply part after the first meeting? Our first impulse would be to answer affirmatively. Yet, on second thought, we are forced to consider whether there may not be *other ways* in which they may become apprised of their partners' latent assets. For example, perhaps the woman is known to some of

* We are not suggesting that either of these two types of men occur frequently, or even that they occur at all. Typically, we would suppose that an individual would hope to find a mate who was a composite of both visible and invisible characteristics. However, the polar types described above are useful, because they enable us to bring certain points into sharp focus.

in an earlier.

their acquaintances, who, in turn, will disclose what she is really like. Certain facets of her character which might otherwise escape early notice will then become known.*

Again, it is commonly recognized that any person involved in a relationship is apt to make many inferences with respect to what the other individual is really like beneath the surface. Moreover, inference-making activity of this type is especially characteristic of the early phases of a relationship (presumably, because at this point the interactors are so "strange" to each other). With respect to the men we are considering here, perhaps certain aspects of the woman's personality, such as her mannerisms, gestures, reactions, etc., will lead them to suspect that she has precisely the features they are looking for.

In conclusion, if we knew more about the external conditions and the interpersonal processes that make an individual less opaque, and if we knew which of the fifty men in the second group (i.e., those who are seeking latent characteristics) would be exposed to these conditions and implicated in these processes, we would, purportedly, have a reasonable basis for predicting which of them would be most likely to become drawn to their partners in the future.†

* The procedures followed by employers in the selection of job applicants are of interest in this context. As is well known, their decision is not apt to depend entirely upon the impression made by an applicant or their knowledge of his job history. In order to discover what he is "really" like, they may solicit the judgment of other people; they may even request the candidate to submit to some kind of psychological testing. Such procedures can be viewed as social mechanisms which have arisen in response to the insistent fact that individuals are initially so opaque.

† It would be especially helpful if we knew more about the workings of the inference-making process referred to, because the characteristics which are imputed, even tentatively, to either partner may vitally affect the course of the relationship. For example, one of our respondents remarked, "My wife was acceptable to me ten minutes after I met her. I do not mean that I was ready to marry her, but she was the type I felt would be suitable for me. . . . I could tell she was a *very decent human being*—it showed in her eyes and in her looks. You could spot it in a minute." What was it that led him to suspect that she was a "decent human being?" For that matter, what is it that leads any of us to suspect that another individual is hypo-

The Partner's Response to the Reluctant

In our previous discussion of how one person (A) may become drawn to another (B), we ignored one highly important aspect about B that may go a long way toward shaping A's feelings toward him: That is, B will react to A in some manner, whether it be with enthusiasm, indifference, or distaste. As a general proposition (for which there is good evidence)[21] we would assume that the more interested B is in A, the more interested will A become in B. Of course, there are exceptions; and we have all been impressed by instances in which A becomes drawn to B, precisely because the latter is so utterly indifferent or disdainful. However, such instances are atypical (and it is their atypicality, no doubt, that makes them so striking.)

There are a number of reasons why we have chosen to deal separately with the partner's mode of response to the Reluctant, rather than grouping it with other features, such as his physical appearance, intelligence, outlook toward life, etc. For one thing, it is likely that almost all people who are looking forward to marriage will hope to find someone who genuinely cares for them. It is perhaps one of the few items that is universally desired, and is thus distinguished from other items which are sought after by some but are of little or no importance to others. Moreover, it is apt to be an exceedingly important marital requirement. In fact, instances in which a woman recognizes that

---

critical, capricious, profound, trustworthy, unselfish, etc.? Are such qualities felt to be revealed by certain distinctive signs?[20]

It would be interesting, in this connection, to study the conditions under which indicators become standardized. (An indicator can be said to be "standardized" when it is commonly believed to signify the presence of particular underlying characteristics. For example, slit eyes and thin lips are generally viewed as indicative of meanness or a calculating attitude.) Perhaps this process of standardization will occur, among other ways, when persons who possess certain latent features in common become anxious to identify each other rapidly and without fail. For example, the distinctive mannerisms of some homosexuals—their gait, gestures, and vocal inflections—would seem to provide rapid and reliable means of identification.

her suitor is deficient in nearly every way, but is drawn to him nonetheless because of his overwhelming interest in her, are not wholly unfamiliar.*

To bring out one further point of differentiation, the characteristics dwelt upon in the preceding passages can be viewed as "belonging" to the individual. They are his "possessions," in the sense that they exist independently— or relatively independently—of the individual with whom he happens to be interacting at the moment. An individual will be handsome or plain, rich or poor, healthy or sickly, talented or untalented, regardless of whom he is exposed to. Of course, not all of his characteristics will be as "independent" as the ones above. For example, while a person may be looked upon as sincere, the degree of his sincerity will be affected by the individual with whom he is currently

---

* In the interviews we conducted there was evidence that, compared to the husbands, the wives were more anxious to find someone who really cared for them. The findings of other studies also suggest that women may place relatively greater emphasis on their partners' responsiveness to them. For example, when Anselm Strauss asked a group of engaged and recently married persons to indicate the needs they would most like to have satisfied in the marital relationship, a greater percentage of the women than of the men wanted "someone to love me."[22]

If these results are typical, the difference in emphasis may be a by-product of the fact that the male and female roles in courtship vary considerably. Unlike the male, the female cannot take the initiative and is therefore at a decided disadvantage when it comes to seeking out someone who possesses the objective characteristics she admires. If, for example, she has her heart set on marrying someone who is handsome, musical, and athletic, she may be frustrated. Accordingly, she may then develop marital aspirations that stand a better chance of being realized. Or perhaps such aspirations have already become institutionalized and are transmitted anew to each female generation. In any event, such an orientation on the part of the female—i.e., the hope of capturing a male who is responsive— would seem to be particularly well adapted to the fact that (roughly speaking) the woman is the one who is chosen and not the one who does the choosing. It is a well-designed adaptation because any male who dates her—however deficient he may be in other respects—automatically reveals an interest in her by this very act. Finally, if our conjectures are correct, and we can imagine a society in which women had the initiative, we would expect a corresponding shift in the things men and women in that society wanted in their mates; more specifically, it would be the men who were more intent upon finding someone who was interested in them.

interacting. Similarly, while a person may be considerd aggressive, his aggressiveness, at any given moment, will be affected by those who are in his presence. Nevertheless, it is convenient, for purposes of our study, to overlook these distinctions and to assume that all of an individual's characteristics will be independent of the specific interpersonal conditions which prevail. In the foregoing discussion we implicitly made use of this model. We suggested that the Reluctants became interested in their partners because the latter possessed ("were the owners of") certain highly prized characteristics, and we then went on to distinguish these features in terms of their initial discernability.

However, the partner's reaction to the Reluctant (or, more generally, B's reaction to A) is a different matter. Whether B responds with enthusiasm, indifference, or distaste will largely depend on the type of person A is. B's reactions will not be constant from one person to another. Accordingly, if B is warmly disposed toward A and A becomes drawn to B as a result, we cannot say that A was attracted by some feature that was an integral part of B's makeup. Rather, A became attracted by a feature which he himself stimulated. Without belaboring the point further, there is enough difference between the partner's so-called objective features and his manner of responding to the Reluctant to warrant treating these two aspects separately.

Unfortunately, this distinction was not made when we drew up the interview questions. That is, while the Reluctants were asked to point out those features in their partners which they had found especially attractive they were not questioned separately about the partner's objective characteristics and his responsiveness. As it turned out, many of the interviewees did not mention how their partners felt about them during various phases of the romance or how their partners' feelings affected their own attitudes. Still, while we cannot go very far toward answering them, there are a couple of questions which are worth raising. First, had the partner demonstrated more interest in the Reluctant than had other persons of his own ethnic group? Second, if the partner had not been more interested, were there any special conditions in the Reluctant's life situation at this point that made whatever interest was demonstrated especially gratifying?

To turn to the first question, there is suggestive evidence that, comparatively speaking, the mate-to-be was more responsive in perhaps half a dozen instances; and that this differentiating feature went a long way toward eliciting the Reluctant's interest:

[CATHOLIC WIFE]: My husband was different from the other fellows I knew because he was shy and nice and sweet. I became serious about him because he was so much nicer to me than other fellows had been. He was respectful. I'd been going with an Italian boy who was not very polite or nice. Herbie was a doll!*

[PROTESTANT WIFE]: I got serious because he persisted so. He seemed to care so much about me.

In another instance, a Catholic husband—married to a Reluctant—said that after catching a glimpse of his wife at a bowling alley, he became "very determined" to meet her. Evidently, he was attracted to her right away: "My wife will not believe this, but I fell in love with her the first time I saw her. When I first met her, I told a Jewish friend of hers that I would marry her." While we cannot assert positively that he was more responsive than her other suitors, it is quite clear that his interest in her did not leave her unaffected. She remarked, "I became drawn to him because he was . . . exceptionally good to me, because he understood me—my feelings and my wishes. For example,

* These remarks were quoted previously in another context.

he was very determined to marry me and didn't even care about giving up his religion."

In all probability, in some cases, it would have been pointless to have asked questions about the relative responsiveness of the individual's dating companions. To be more specific, there were several Reluctant women in our group who would not be rated very desirable as dates and whose chances of getting married at all were probably rather limited. Because they had been by-passed so frequently before, any interest shown in them was probably especially appreciated and immediately returned. We strongly suspect this was so in the following case of a Jewish woman, who was in her middle thirties when she met her husband at a public dance and lecture:

I wouldn't let him take me home the night we met. I was tired and my friend had forced me to go to the dance anyway. However, he called me the next day to find out if I got home all right. I was *impressed* that he remembered my name without writing it down, and had to call a couple of girls with my name before he got me. I thought that was *nice* and *unusual.* . . .You should have seen what he did for my birthday [*before they were married*]. I was at my sister's and he sent candy and flowers [*with sighs and exclamations over the cost*] and I knew he couldn't afford it!

At this point let us suppose that all the Reluctants had been asked to compare the degree of interest manifested in them by their various dating companions, and that we discovered that their mates had *not* been more absorbed in them than had some of their other partners. Would this mean that no special significance could be attributed to the interest actually displayed in them by their future mates? Not necessarily. Special conditions may well have made their responsiveness, coming at the time it did, especially gratifying. In brief, an individual's emotional vulnerability to others is not a constant, but will depend on his life situation at the moment. At a given period he may be in particular need of affection and support, and if these are forthcoming at this time, he may become strongly drawn to the donor. For example, someone who has been "jilted" may be particularly susceptible to the attention of others in the period immediately following this experience.

When we examined the histories of the Reluctants with these thoughts in mind, we noted that two of our subjects had been in a state of emotional turmoil when they met their future husbands. One of these, a Jewish woman, remarked, "My mother had just died. I had gone through a terrific ordeal. I was in sort of a mess then." Quite possibly, her partner's interest in her at this point of her life played a more vital role than would otherwise have been the case. More suggestive in this connection were the remarks of the other Reluctant, a Catholic girl, who had been attracted to her husband because, among other reasons, he was "sympathetic" and "understanding":

At the time I met Henry I was exceedingly unhappy at home. I was at my wit's end and really down in the dumps. Henry felt he had to stand by me during this time because of what I might do if I didn't have him to lean on. He was the rock of Gibraltar to me.

The remarks of an Amenable Protestant wife, who had not been impressed by her husband initially, are also relevant:

He was *so kind* to me at the time of Dad's death and was a real bulwark. He did lots of things that he didn't have to do for me and helped me out. Right after Dad's death I saw him all the time, almost every night, because I thought I was going off my rocker. Also, after our auto accident in February, he literally took care of me. I was living alone and he'd come over and make breakfast for me and then lunch, too. Of course, I loved all this; I was a terribly spoiled child anyway.*

Aside from the two Reluctants noted above, we have no evidence that any other of our Reluctant subjects had been emotionally distraught when they met their future mates. However, we should remind ourselves at this point of an obvious, but significant, fact: It is very probable that many, if not all, of the Reluctants did become emotionally disturbed as their romances progressed. They were in an acute conflict situation: they were drawn to their partners and at the same time they wished to retreat. There is no question that this type of situation can produce marked anxiety:

[JEWISH WIFE]: My mother was opposed to my going out with George and getting serious, until about March. During that time I required a doctor because I was so nervous and upset. My mother wouldn't discuss the problem of George with me, and it was the first time we had not been able to talk things over and be open and frank with each other. This made me so upset that finally I went to a doctor—our old family doctor we had known for many years. . . . The doctor told my mother this was all leading to the point where I was ready for a nervous breakdown.

What consequences did the anxiety which the Reluctants experienced (presumably) have for their affairs? No

---

* Perhaps there is still another way in which a crisis situation may serve to promote a courtship (i.e., aside from the fact that it may render one of the partners more vulnerable emotionally). As is commonly recognized, the courtship setting is apt to be characterized by a certain degree of mutual distrust. Particularly in the early phases of an affair, each of the interactors is apt to cast a wary eye upon the other and wonder how sincere the other's declarations of affection actually are. However, if partner A is emotionally distraught for some reason, such a situation would seem to provide B with an unusual opportunity for conveying the genuineness of his feelings. By being sympathetic and understanding—more generally, by offering support—he can reveal the sincerity of his feelings more effectively. Conversely, in the absence of a crisis situation, A might continue to question, and for some period of time, how B really feels about him.

doubt their inner turmoil deterred them from becoming involved, and it is easy to see why they might have solved their predicament by simply breaking off the romance. But these individuals did get married, and the question arises as to whether their feelings of stress—while, above all, a deterrent—might not have simultaneously promoted the romance in certain indirect ways. One suspects that as the Reluctant became increasingly distraught, quite possibly, his need for someone to affirm a genuine interest in him and to offer him support became correspondingly greater. Under such conditions, the partner's interest (or absorption) in him may have been especially gratifying and may have served to draw him even closer to his partner. We get a hint of some such process in the following case. It concerns a Jewish fiancée, who was quite upset by the antagonism of her parents (who, among other things, were threatening to disown her):

[*Why did you become attracted to your fiancé?*] I didn't feel guarded when I talked to him. For instance, I told him about how my parents felt, and he was very understanding. . . . My fiancé seemed to have so much understanding that I could tell him anything I felt, and this was one of the reasons I began to get serious about him.

The type of process to which we are alluding is indeed curious. It is curious because it was the Reluctant himself who was responsible for generating his emotional instability and, in turn, for creating those very conditions that ultimately led him to become increasingly drawn to his partner. We cannot attribute his emotional instability to some outside disaster which had suddenly befallen him, such as a death in the family. Rather, by continuing to perform the "forbidden" act (i.e., to see his partner), he was leading himself into a state of anguish and thereby rendering himself more receptive to the interest shown in him by his **partner.**

To summarize this chapter very briefly, we have been concerned with the phenomena which enabled the Reluctants, despite their early awareness of their partners' ethnic affiliation, to become sufficiently interested in them to date. In trying to grapple with this problem, the process of "becoming attracted" was divided into two components: A's attraction to B was visualized as a function of the objective characteristics possessed by B and of B's response to A. It was suggested that the Reluctants became attracted to their partners for any one, or all, of the following reasons: Their partners had possessed—and to a greater degree than their previous ingroup dating partners—certain highly prized objective characteristics (whether these happened to be of an initially visible type or not); their partners manifested more interest in them than had dating partners from the ingroup; their partners' interest was manifested at a time when it was especially appreciated.

5 . . . The Concept of a Stationary Relationship

IN THE preceding two chapters an effort was made to account for the fact that the Reluctants became "interested" in their partners. Of course, strictly speaking, some of the subjects' comments and our interpretations have bearing on why the Reluctants subsequently became "involved," rather than just "interested." However, it is essential to recognize that the Reluctant's feelings for his partner might not have progressed beyond the stage of "interest." It was not inevitable that his feelings would become stronger; no doubt, there are many persons, similar to those in our group, who broke off before reaching the involvement stage. In this and the following chapter, we shall dwell upon some of the conditions which appear to have been responsible for the movement of the Reluctant's feelings from the plateau of interest to the plateau of involvement.

It must be stated first that by dividing the romance into

the stages of interest and involvement we are not implying that our subjects experienced a sudden intensification in their feelings for each other—that they were "interested" on Tuesday and "involved" on Wednesday. Typically, their sentiments developed slowly and over a considerable period of time. Furthermore, it is not suggested that influences dealt with previously, and those still to be considered, operated only at specified intervals; rather, influences which operated at one phase also operated at others. Nevertheless, some factors appear to have been of greater importance at certain stages. To consider these in context, it is useful to divide the process of falling in love into the phases of interest and involvement.

When the Reluctants first met their partners, it is very unlikely that they thought they would ever become seriously involved. What is of greater interest, at least half a dozen (and perhaps many more) remained convinced that nothing serious would develop even after their interest had become aroused. They felt the relationship would remain stationary, that their ties would not become more intimate. When we were analyzing our data at the conclusion of the interview stage, those of their remarks which bore on this topic drew our attention—particularly since they were spontaneous and not in response to specific questions we had posed:

[PROTESTANT HUSBAND]: For the first six or eight months I enjoyed going with her, but had no serious intentions of getting seriously involved. . . . I was really kind of a snob. When I was first dating her, I felt I couldn't get interested in a girl without a college education or a Jew.

[CATHOLIC HUSBAND]: About a month after we met, we went steady and we liked each other a lot. . . . But I didn't think it would become serious. At the time, I didn't know this would happen. At the time, I was just going out and enjoying myself.

[CATHOLIC WIFE]: Yes, I certainly felt hesitant about becoming involved with a Jew, but I thought nothing would happen. I thought it would be kind of fun to have a beau in the office. If I had any inkling of what was going to happen, I never would have seen him again.

Conversely, the realization that a marriage might occur led to a temporary breakup in the following case:

[CATHOLIC WIFE]: After graduation, that's when we really thought seriously about marriage. We broke up after we thought about it. I thought then something could be done, but there was so much pressure put on both of us that I felt it wasn't worth it. There were too many people involved—too many people were going to feel hurt.

An additional five Reluctants spontaneously voiced the opinion that, in their eyes, the possibility of a marriage had seemed remote indeed:

[JEWISH HUSBAND]: [*Did you continue to feel hesitant about becoming involved?*] Yes, I became more conscious of the fact that our religions were different. The matter of religion came up between the two of us. We never imagined that we would be married.

[JEWISH WIFE]: I still don't know where I got the nerve to pack up and leave and go and get married. I was such a protected child. I just remember I felt a blank, with no feelings, no emotions, the day I left home. I had always told Walter we'd never have the nerve to get married.

Actually, we do not know whether the two Reluctants just quoted, like those quoted earlier, had believed that their *feelings* would not become more profound as the courtship progressed. They (as well as three others) said only that they felt a *marriage* would not occur. Nevertheless, for purposes of discussion, we shall assume that they, too, had conceived of the relationship as stationary, in the sense that at the point when they were "just interested" in their partners, they believed that their feelings would not move beyond this level.*

What led certain of the Reluctants to believe that their feelings for their partners would not become stronger? And what is even more important, what consequences did these expectations have for their affairs? For an obvious reason, data bearing on these topics were not solicited. Not until we had read the transcripts of the interviews did we become provoked by comments such as those quoted above —comments which, in turn, led us to formulate the questions stated above. Because we did not solicit information bearing upon them, we are in a position which is familiar enough to those who conduct exploratory studies, namely, we are acutely aware of our need for more data. Still, it is worthwhile to consider the questions noted in further detail, with the aid of the information we did secure, since there is reason to believe the Reluctant's image of the "end" of his affair played a significant role in bringing about his marriage.

Presumably, the Reluctants' notion that nothing serious would evolve as a result of their relationship with their partners was in some measure an outgrowth of their general resistance to intermarriage. Because the Reluctant was so unwilling to become involved with (or to marry) someone

---

* There was an Amenable Jewish male in our group who, curiously enough, did not seem to have any expectations whatsoever as to where his affair might lead: "I never had any thoughts about marriage. I'm quite serious—I never gave the matter any thought. As far as marriage was concerned, I felt it was inevitable, like certain other things. I felt it was best just not to bother pondering about things like this. . . . One day I just found myself trapped." It would seem that this boy had been completely present-oriented: He neither envisioned that he would become involved with his wife, nor did he envision he would *not* become involved with her. To borrow a phrase from Morris Rosenberg, individuals of this type might appropriately be labeled "myopics"—as distinct from those who are "farsighted."[1]

who was different ethnically, he probably automatically "ruled out" his partner as a mate. However, because it is so general, such an observation is not very helpful. It is not very helpful because the short-term perspective of *any* Reluctant in the population could probably be traced back to the same conditions. What we want to know here is whether there were any additional conditions which led the Reluctants we interviewed to believe their cross-ethnic relationships would remain stationary.

To begin with, as mentioned previously, several of our Reluctant subjects were simply not in the marriage market at the time at which they met their future mates (e.g., a boy of sixteen, and a middle-aged widow who had no intention of ever remarrying). Presumably, these individuals did not expect to become seriously attached to the person they were dating, because they did not expect to become seriously attached to anyone. But what about those Reluctants who were looking forward to marriage in the near future? What were their grounds for believing that the affair, once it was under way, would not become more serious? There were several Reluctants who, although they found their partners appealing, did not find them appealing enough to consider them seriously as matrimonial possibilities:

[PROTESTANT WIFE]: Although I felt I cared for him, I wasn't sure I wanted to marry him. He wrote me for a long time when he was away and phoned me a lot too. However, I was hesitant about writing him. Anyway, I corresponded with him during October. [*Why did you change your mind about writing to him?*] Maybe I thought I'd write to him because I was sure I wouldn't marry him. And I decided that there wasn't that much to be afraid of—that I probably wouldn't come to care that much for him anyway.

[JEWISH WIFE]: My first impression was that I thought him nice, but I didn't particularly care for him. It was not love at first sight. He was terribly shy. . . . When he finally asked me for a date, I saw him for two weeks regularly. Then I decided I wouldn't see him any more. [*Why?*] Because I didn't care for him. But I felt sorry for him—he was so shy—and when he asked me for another date, I couldn't say no. . . . Yes, I guess I did feel hesitant at first. I didn't want to marry outside of my religion. But I wasn't too hesitant, because I wasn't afraid of getting involved. [*Why was that?*] Because I thought I didn't love him at all.

It is interesting to note that even if the Reluctant does find his partner very attractive, he may still feel assured that nothing serious will develop. He may feel that he is in complete command of his emotions. In this connection, a Jewish male, when asked whether he had anticipated that he might marry out of his faith, replied:

Well, let me put it this way—I thought that it was possible, but I did not seriously think it could happen. I had been going with Gentile girls, and I was aware that it could happen, but I felt that *I would not let it happen to me.*

The individuals just quoted believed that they could prevent their partners' attractive features from making too great an emotional impression, or that their partners were not attractive enough to be considered marital prospects. There were still other reasons which led the Reluctants to believe they would not become more attached. Several apparently felt that their partners' intentions were not serious:

[JEWISH FIANCÉE]: I felt it was probably just a fling on his part—you know, like the sailor who has a girl in every port. He took me home that night after we met . . . and said, "When can I see you again?" and I said, "Oh, any time," thinking he didn't mean it. Then he said, "How about tomorrow?" I was so surprised, I said O.K. He didn't know his way around New York at all, and I felt it was all really a huge joke, and he'd never even find his way back again to take me out. Even my mother laughed when I told her about it.

[CATHOLIC WIFE]: From the beginning, he said he would never marry me, so relax and forget about that angle.

Once the Reluctants believed their affairs would remain stationary—whatever the basis for this conviction—what led them to continue the relationship? For one thing, they were interested in their partners; they liked them and enjoyed their company. Nevertheless, there is certainly a tendency on the part of those who are looking forward to marriage to discontinue an affair that appears to have no "future." As an Amenable Jewish husband remarked, "I wanted more from the relationship. . . . I said to my wife, 'Let's quit writing to each other, if it's only going to come to this.'"

We might speculate as to why those Reluctants for whom the affair could only lead to a dead-end prolonged it. A Jewish woman (whose remarks were cited earlier) was the only Reluctant to express herself on this subject:

When he finally asked me for a date, I saw him for two weeks regularly. Then I decided I wouldn't see him any more. [*Why?*] Because I didn't care for him. But I felt sorry for him—he was so shy—and when he asked me for another date, I couldn't say no.

Undoubtedly, there were other reasons why the Reluctants did not disassociate themselves from their partners. As noted earlier, some of the Reluctant couples found themselves in the same organizational setting; others were surrounded by mutual friends. Under such circumstances, the Reluctant may have felt constrained to continue the affair; he may have felt he could not easily detach himself without suffering embarrassing consequences: ("I considered breaking off, but I didn't know how to get out of it.")

Again, a few may have had ulterior motives for continuing the relationship. Perhaps the men hoped to gain sexual favors (as was certainly true in at least one case). As for the women, perhaps they were anxious to be seen out or were hopeful of meeting other men through their partners.

In review, it has been pointed out that the Reluctants (at least some of them) believed that their feelings for their partners would not become more intense. Looking ahead, they did not foresee any danger. These expectations—when considered in conjunction with other conditions (though these are largely unknown)—led them to go on dating. At this point let us consider whether the fact that the partners continued to date affected their feelings for each other and/or the likelihood of their marriage.

To begin with, the very fact that these people went on seeing each other led to a continuation of the process previously depicted. That is, as the members of the dyad continued to interact, more of their latent assets became exposed to view. And as the Reluctants recognized more fully what their partners were really like, they became more deeply attached to them.

At this juncture, let us turn our attention to courtships in the wider population. Apart from the partners' greater insight into each other's "sterling" qualities, there are other factors which may increase the likelihood of a marriage. For one, because the two see so much of each other, they become increasingly cut off from other prospective marital partners. This, in turn, may lead them to become more dependent upon each other.

To analyze this process in detail, the partners are apt to become cut off from other marital prospects for several reasons. First, as they continue to see more of each other, they will probably find they are dating other acquaintances much less frequently. While this may be a matter of choice, lack of time, in itself, may prevent them from maintaining former ties: ("I was seeing Bill five or six times a week during this period, so there really wasn't time to see anyone else.") At the same time, other contacts may infer, either from personal observation or from gossip they have heard, that the individual is no longer romantically accessible. Accordingly, they are likely to withdraw. In short, as a result of these processes, the individual will become increasingly dissociated from those he had formerly dated.

In addition, by devoting his time increasingly to one person, the individual reduces the likelihood that relationships will form between himself and other persons who are currently unknown to him, but who might be eligible marital prospects. Perhaps he will actively discourage any friendly overtures from "newcomers." Or these so-called newcomers may look elsewhere for dates, not because they have made advances and been rebuffed, but because it is their impression (which may or may not be correct) that the individual in question is not available. In short, the members of the dyad—by continuing to see a lot of each other (and particularly if they become engaged)—intentionally and/or unintentionally create a situation in which they become increasingly isolated from other marital possibilities.*

* It should be added that the actor may become even more cut off if he is going around with someone looked upon in his circle as being utterly reprehensible. Members of the opposite sex in his milieu may draw back, not just because he is out of circulation, so to speak, but because he has "soiled" himself in their eyes. For example, one can imagine a situation in which a white girl's consorting with a Negro would result in a lowering of her marital desirability. Roberts, who interviewed a great many interracial couples in Chicago, remarks: "The stigma attached to the White person who has married a Negro remains after the colored spouse dies or is divorced. If a White woman loses her Negro husband, she is more likely to marry another Negro than a White man if she remarries. . . . A number of White wives I interviewed said that once you marry a Negro you are in the colored group for life."[2] The second interracial marriage on the part of these white women was perhaps a by-product, in part, of their having disqualified themselves in the eyes of potential white suitors. Generalizing this idea, we might say that behavior which departs from the norms of a group is promoted when individuals in the actor's milieu, whose presence might result in such deviant tendencies being curbed, draw away from the actor because they are offended by his conduct.

We have yet to consider why the partners' increasing isolation from other marital prospects should lead them to become more dependent upon each other. Perhaps the fact that there are now fewer "alternatives" on the horizon will lead their feelings for each other to become more intense. This is not to say, of course, that their chances of becoming involved are nil if they continue to be surrounded by a host of attractive persons who are actively interested in them. We are merely suggesting that when two such individuals are out of circulation, there will be more likelihood of their falling in love.

However, let us suppose that the partners' being out of circulation has *not* intensified their feelings for each other. Let us also suppose that, as they continue to go around together, one or both become increasingly doubtful as to whether the other is actually "right" for him. When this is the case, we would certainly agree with the following observation: "Sometimes there is the feeling that too much has been invested in even an unsatisfactory relationship to justify its rupture. One gambles, as it were, on the possibility of success in the old relationship because of one's share in the 'jackpot'."[3] In this context we might say that the more isolated the partners have become, the more wary will they be of a rupture, and the more likely will they be to gamble upon the relationship's future. Presumably, their stakes are greater, because at this point their alternatives have become more limited and they have less chance of locating a promising replacement. Accordingly, rather than risk the uncertainties of breaking off, they may tend to push their apprehensions aside and go through with the marriage. Here again we might say that the partners' increasing isolation led them to become more dependent upon each other—however, not in the sense that they had become more involved emotionally (as in the instance first considered), but in the sense that their getting married at all had become increasingly dependent upon the course taken by their immediate affair.

As a matter of everyday experience,[4] we know that if either party to a man-woman relationship becomes interested in someone else, this may lead to the end of the affair. But with reference to relationships that do not break up, the effects of the fact that the partners are out of circulation —that they are cut off from other marital prospects—are apt to be overlooked. It is their isolation from others that makes it less likely that either of them will become interested in someone else. Were it not for some such process, such relationships, presumably, would dissolve more frequently than they actually do.*

To place the foregoing discussion in the context of our study, let us suppose we could compare the courtships of the Reluctants in our group with the romances of Reluctants who became interested in cross-ethnics but did not marry them. From what has been said, we would expect these courtships to differ in certain ways. We would expect to find that our interviewees had become more cut off from persons they had formerly dated; and more removed from potential prospects (for the reasons noted). We would further anticipate that their greater isolation had promoted their marriages.

Let us consider one final question. We suggested that the Reluctant's conviction that he would not become more attached was one of the elements which led him, counter

* Willard Waller's depiction of mate selection as an irreversible process is relevant in this context: "Each of the successive steps in the process of mating is more powerfully determined by social pressures and inner impulse than the one which preceded it. As the process unfolds, each person becomes increasingly committed in his own eyes and those of others to the completed act, and at the same time his impulses are increasingly stirred up. Once they have reached a level of a certain intensity, these relations have a movement of their own which is more or less beyond the control of individuals. The social process of mating tends to be irreversible after it has gained a certain momentum."[5] We would suggest that the irreversibility of this process is, in part, an outcome of the partners' increasing isolation from other marital prospects.

to his expectations, to become more attached. Turning this around, what effect did his increasing attachment have upon his earlier outlook? For example, did the "facts" of the situation lead him to abandon his belief that the affair would remain stationary? Or is it possible that he went on believing—and perhaps for some time—that nothing serious would develop, while actually he was becoming more involved all the time? Stated in this manner, it might appear that the Reluctants simply misjudged what was happening. Obviously, this does occur, and maybe it was the case with respect to some of the Reluctants in our group. In some instances, their feelings for the other may have evolved so slowly and undramatically that they were scarcely aware of transitions in the relationship: ("We were not a big romance—we just drifted together as we got to know each other.") Again, maybe the emotional attachment built up gradually, below the level of awareness, until suddenly, a point of recognition was reached. Instances in which individuals are shocked into the realization of the intensity of their feelings for another are certainly not unknown, as witness the remarks of one of our respondents: "Sam and I had been in an automobile accident together. When I woke up and thought I'd killed him, I realized I was serious about him."* Finally, it may be that the Reluctant progressively redefined the future. While he realized that his feelings had become stronger and had broken through the limits earlier projected, he may have periodically reassured himself that things would go no further in the future.

We have been unable to say very much about the specific Reluctants in our group with respect to the topics discussed in this chapter. This was inevitable, since at the time the interviews were conducted, our respondents' expectations

* This type of occurrence, as well as other processes involved in what are referred to as "transformations of identity," have been discussed by Anselm Strauss.[6]

during courtship of what the future might hold, and the consequent effect of these expectations, were of no concern to us. It was only after the interviews had been completed and we had gone over the material many times that it appeared that the Reluctants' image of the future might have played a significant role in leading their feelings to move from the "interest" stage to the "involvement" stage. We then went on to conjecture about the nature of this process in greater detail and to set forth a number of related questions.

While some investigators might argue that only processes which can be documented should be discussed in an interview study such as this, we believe that posing questions may prove of value, even though they cannot be answered on the basis of the empirical data at hand. For by raising questions, one directs attention to problem areas which may prove worthy of investigation.

6 . . .   *The Partner's*

"Concessions"

AT THIS JUNCTURE let us move back to an earlier stage and look at these romances at the point at which the Reluctant was "interested" in his partner. The Reluctant was confronted by the incontrovertible fact that his partner was not a Jew (or a Christian) like himself. If he were to become seriously involved in the relationship and a marriage were to result, what would his new family's orientation toward religion be, and how would the family be identified socially in the eyes of others? Would his own religious affiliation and social identity prevail, or would his partner's ethnic background prevail? Understandably, these questions were a source of anxiety for our subjects and blocked their feelings for their partners from developing freely and/or reduced the likelihood of a marriage. From what we could gather, most of the Reluctant's apprehensions centered upon the children he and his partner might have in the future:

[CATHOLIC FIANCÉE]: While deciding to get married I was upset. My fiance and I both went through a long period of personal emotional disturbance—especially about the children and what religion they should be.

[JEWISH WIFE]: I felt that with different religions the one big problem was that the couple must get together, and there must be one religion only in the family. This is important because the children must know definitely what they are, not just that they are half and half.

A Jewish male, who "could never give up his Jewish identity," remarked:

What made me feel hesitant about becoming involved . . . was the very real fact of the difficulties involved—the question of the children and the question of cultural differences in marriage. We felt we were similar, we agreed on many things. Yet there was this difference, and it did become a problem. . . . This is one of the things that held us up.

In this chapter we shall confine ourselves, for the most part, to questions having to do with the couple's future children, and we shall divide these questions into two subtypes: those having to do with the children's religious orientation and those having to do with their social identity. While these two aspects are inter-related, we shall deal with them separately (and in the order named) in order to draw attention to certain differences between them.

The Children's Religious Orientation

By way of preliminary discussion, let us consider a very general question. Is there any *possible* solution to the religious-cultural problem from the standpoint of those who are reluctant to marry out of their ethnic group? Is the barrier that separates the partners immutable, forever destined to remain a divisive force? Clearly, this need not be the case. The Reluctant's partner, if he is so inclined, can accede to the religious demands of the other and thus remove certain impediments to the marriage.

It will be recognized that not all types of barriers that separate two marriageable persons are as soluble. In fact, some barriers are unalterable (in a structural sense). For example, an individual's resistance to marriage may stem from the fact that his woman friend is ten years his senior. If her age continues to be a "thorn in his side," there is no possibility of this obstacle being removed. Obviously, even though she may be more than willing to do so, the woman is quite unable to alter her chronological age. However, if it is her religion that is causing difficulty, she can appease the man by converting to his faith or by agreeing, at least, to subordinate her religion to his in the marriage.

Such an accommodation is possible because religion, unlike age, is not a biologically fixed entity. But, in addition, it is important to note that the social structure *permits* the two partners to arbitrate the issue. Of course, there is nothing inevitable about this. Theoretically, the social structure could prescribe the course to be followed, but it does not. As a result, the partners themselves are socially empowered to determine the outcome.

With these preliminary remarks in mind (i.e., that the Reluctants in our group were concerned about the religion in which their children would be reared and that mixed couples, *per se*, are invested with the authority to resolve this issue), let us jump ahead to a point shortly before these couples were married and see what course, if any, they had agreed to follow. Ignoring for the present four couples where both members were Reluctants, there were twenty-one pairs in which one member was a Reluctant and the other was not. With reference to this group—and omitting an engaged couple who were still debating the issue—in sixteen instances the Amenable agreed, during the premarital phase, to raise the children in the Reluctant's faith, while in four instances no explicit decision was reached. In brief, the Reluctant's religion, whether Jewish or Christian, typically prevailed. That this was more than a "fluke" is suggested by the course followed by those couples where both members were Amenables. Here the decision (when one was reached) was as likely to go one way as the other. Neither the Jewish nor Christian tradition was favored.

First, let us turn to the sixteen Reluctant-Amenable couples where the Amenable member agreed to have the offspring reared in the other's faith. While it is true that these "agreements" varied in terms of how firmly the Amenable committed himself, it is worth noting that in fourteen of these cases the marriage ceremony was performed in the Reluctant's religion. (A civil ceremony was performed in the other two instances.)

What consequences did these concessions have for the Reluctant? Frequently, the end result was to remove an obstacle which had blocked the development of his feelings for his partner.

[JEWISH WIFE]: I continued to feel hesitant about becoming involved until the problems of the marriage ceremony and the children were settled, and then I allowed myself to become serious about him.

[CATHOLIC WIFE]: I changed [became less hesitant about becoming involved with a Jew] because Len and I spoke about it together, and he agreed to be married in a Catholic church and bring up the children Catholic.

In short, the Amenable's compliance in instances such as these helps to explain why the Reluctant's feelings toward his partner moved from interest to involvement.

On several occasions, the Reluctant was seriously involved *before* questions regarding the future were resolved (although they were resolved before the marriage). A Jewish husband remarked:

I felt extremely hesitant about becoming involved with her for a long time. [*Did you continue to feel this way or did you change?*] There was no change. What occurred was that I was in love with her and she was in love with me.

How did this man, in contrast to others, happen to fall in love before the religious question was settled? Perhaps he felt that when the time came to broach the topic, his partner would see things his way or at least yield in the end. In other words, if he had suspected that his partner might be obdurate, it is perhaps less likely he would have fallen in love. In this connection, one of the Amenables in our group remarked, "I never hesitated about getting involved with Jewish boys in general, except if their attitudes on religion and on rearing the children were very strict."

While the effect of these religious concessions varied, in one way or another they all promoted the marriage. Accordingly, it is pertinent to ask just why these decisions were made in favor of the Reluctant. Basically, the outcome stemmed from the fact that, of the two, the Reluctant was more committed to his religion (whether "personally" or because of his parents):

[CATHOLIC WIFE]: We are going to bring up any children Catholic. I was brought up Catholic and I feel it's the true religion. Although my husband was Bar Mitzvah, he was never really brought up in a religion. He never went to synagogue or anything. . . . Peter didn't exactly suggest they be brought up Catholic, but he knew I wanted it and he said, after all, he would be no example for them to follow.

[PROTESTANT WIFE]: Our children are going to be brought up as Christians. . . . I have a strong belief that you have to believe in Christ. The Jewish religion is beautiful, from what I know, but

the Protestant religion is stronger in this family. . . . We talked
about this before we were married, and Leon said he didn't
feel pro-Jewish. He had been to Presbyterian church a lot with
his first wife and thought this was a good faith for our children.

[JEWISH FIANCÉE]: We have decided to bring our children up
Jewish. . . . My fiancé is only one child out of five in his family
and I am the only one in my family, so we felt it would help to
reconcile my parents to me and what I had done, and it wouldn't
make so much difference to his parents.

[JEWISH HUSBAND]:* The identity of the child will undoubtedly
be Jewish—this is pretty well settled. [*How does your wife feel
about this?*] At the present time she agrees. At first she hoped
we could find some ideal atmosphere where religious differences
would make no difference. But this is not really achievable.
Since this is so, she is willing to bring them up with a Jewish
identity. [*Did you discuss bringing the children up in your
wife's religion?*] Yes, but she realized that I could never give up
my Jewish identity. [*Did you find this a difficult decision to
make?*] Not terribly. It soon became obvious what the answer
had to be.†

* This couple had been married for two months.
† The determination of Jews to have their children raised in their religion may be reinforced by their fear that, lacking such training, their
children will be engulfed by the majority culture. For example, a Jewish
wife, who hoped her children would be raised in her faith, remarked:
"Unless the children have some Jewish education, they won't feel Jewish
because they will probably live in a non-Jewish environment." To better
understand this process, let us suppose that the child's primary environment as he grows up is internally divided, and that the Jewish and Gentile
sides of the family exert equal pressure upon him to assume their orientation. How this cross-pressure situation will be resolved may be influenced
by the fact that, generally speaking, the culture surrounding the child is
more apt to be non-Jewish. Other things being equal, this contextual influence may tip the scales, leading a disproportionate number of such
children to orient toward the Christian culture.
    The views just expressed were prompted by a study of voting behavior.
The authors suggest—and provide supporting evidence—that when individuals whose personal associates are politically divided live in a community that is Republican, the surrounding environment will lead a disproportionate number of them to vote Republican. They refer to this as
the "breakage" effect.[1]

Let us turn to some other cases which further illustrate that, of the two, the Reluctant was more ardent about his faith. In these instances, the Reluctant informed his partner that if the latter did not accede to his demands, the marriage simply would not take place:

[RELUCTANT CATHOLIC WIFE]: The children will be brought up Catholic. We discussed this before we were married. My husband had to sign a paper agreeing to bring the children up Catholic. My religion is too strong for me ever to have considered anything else. . . . No compromise choice was possible.

[HER HUSBAND]: I could not have been married if I did not agree to raise the children as Catholics. . . . My wife once said that if it were a choice of me or her religion, it would be her religion.

[RELUCTANT JEWISH HUSBAND]: As for my wife's conversion—I wanted her to convert, *it was a condition of the marriage*. . . . Having her convert was my way of feeling at home with myself about this whole matter. If I did not marry within my own group, the least I could do was to bring my wife into the fold. I suppose I have a kind of peculiar pride about being Jewish.

[HIS WIFE]: I was willing and anxious to convert. I had never been a great Catholic, and there were many things about Catholicism I could never accept. I found in Judaism many things I had believed in all along, and it seemed silly not to become a Jew. . . . I felt absolutely no regrets about giving up Catholicism. There were so many questions it couldn't answer to my satisfaction, and there had been for many years.*

* When one considers that the structure of Catholicism is monolithic while Judaism and Protestantism, on the other hand, are composed of many sects or denominations, one might be tempted to hypothesize that alienated Catholics would be more likely to convert to some other faith than would alienated Jews or Protestants. The latter groups, unless they are completely estranged from everything that Judaism or Protestantism represents, may still find it possible to remain within the boundaries of their own creed: Orthodox Jews may find Reform Judaism more appeal-

The fact that each partner was not committed to his faith with equal intensity was of crucial importance in accounting for the religious decisions noted above. However, other elements contributed to the Reluctant's "victory" as well. To bring those into focus, we shall turn first to some comments made by the Reluctants' partners. Two of these partners—both Catholic wives—were intent upon having *some kind* of religious ceremony. Since they could not be married by a priest, they preferred to have a Jewish wedding rather than a civil ceremony:

I wanted a religious ceremony, and it was important to me. I felt the civil ceremony was cold and had no spiritual character—that it was purely legal. Obviously, no priest would marry us. . . . And my husband said if we were going to have a religious ceremony, he wanted a rabbi.

Why was I converted to Judaism? I wanted to be married in a church. I wanted to be married in the eyes of God, and how could I be married by a priest? So I decided to convert. I converted so we could be married by a rabbi.

On one occasion, it was the partner's parents who wanted a religious ceremony, even if it had to be performed in the "wrong" religion:

---

ing; Methodists may become Unitarians. However, estranged Catholics are not given the opportunity to "circulate" within the fold and may have to look elsewhere for religious beliefs and practices which are compatible with their convictions.

On the other hand, any tendency on the part of an alienated Catholic to convert may be countered by another force. Catholic dogma, such as the horrors of life in the hereafter if one is excommunicated, may deter even an emancipated Catholic from leaving his church. If these conjectures are correct, we might say that, from a structural point of view, Catholicism maintains control over its members through the severity of its indoctrination, while Judaism and Protestantism maintain control by providing a range of alternatives for those who have become dissatisfied with their particular sects.

[CATHOLIC HUSBAND]: I told my parents that we would get married civil—that is, just go to City Hall. My mother did not like that. She said that I ought to get married the right way. I ought to have some type of religious ceremony. Another reason she suggested a Jewish ceremony was because of my wife's parents—so that they would not be offended.

A Jewish husband (Amenable) was anxious for his children to have a strong religious upbringing—an upbringing which he could not provide because of his lack of familiarity with Judaism as such, but which his Catholic wife (Reluctant) could provide:

Eighty-five percent of my worries are about the children becoming bums. When I walk out of that door in the morning, I want to be able to feel that everything will be all right when I come back. . . . I have a lot of friends who have been in jail. I think part of the trouble was that they did not have religion. I think the chances are better that our children will stay out of trouble if they have a strong religious background. They will have to answer to that Guy up there. There will be someone else besides me and my wife to keep them in line.

To return to the Reluctants, it is curious to note that whether they happened to be males or females—and, consequently, prospective fathers or mothers—they argued for the supremacy of their religion by appealing to their respective roles as parents. For instance, a Jewish husband explained why his faith would be dominant as follows: "A house where the father is Jewish and the children have a different identity is very confusing." The Catholic wife of a Reluctant, whose children will be raised as Jews, declared it was her husband's right to make the choice: "My husband's the man of the family and he's Jewish, and it's his privilege to bring them up. It's his choice to make."

However, some of the Reluctant wives expressed quite a different opinion:

[JEWISH WIFE]: Our children will be brought up Jewish. I feel children should always be the mother's religion, because the mother is with them all day. . . . I just think the children should be the mother's religion regardless of what she is.

[JEWISH WIFE]: The reasons for deciding to raise the children Jewish were the mother has more influence over the child in religious matters and teaches the child more, and I wouldn't know what else to teach them.

It was precisely the fear of the mother's influence over the child that led the Jewish husband quoted below to stop seeing his Catholic girl friend temporarily:

I was strongly in favor of the children being raised Jewish, and I was fearful that if this were not undertaken that automatically, by nature of the mother-child relationship, the children would be raised and identified Catholic. There was a strong reaction on my wife's part at the time, a feeling of being lost. . . . There was a feeling on my part that my wife would not be able to raise the children as Jewish. This was the cause of our break. . . . A week and a half later she said that she could raise the children Jewish and have a Jewish home. . . . The conviction was strong within her that she could do this. We were both very much in love with each other—we called the rabbi and made a date to be married.

There is no empirical evidence, at least to our knowledge, as to whether members of the population feel children of mixed parentage *should* be raised in the mother's religion or in the father's religion.* However, we would guess that if an opinion survey were undertaken, the results would reveal no great consensus. It seems as though certain cultural norms invest the father with the authority to take command, while others place the necessary authority in

* It might also be added that very little is known about the course that is actually followed. What little information is available for this country —and it does not permit wide generalization—suggests that the mother's religion is more apt to be dominant.[2]

the hands of the mother. In this connection, it is worth noting the remarks of one of our subjects (who had been married two years and whose comments pertain to her current feelings). One senses that the lack of clear definition with respect to this decision-making activity was responsible, in part, for her indecision and uneasiness:

[PROTESTANT WIFE]: My husband does not want any religious education for the children. . . . I don't know as I would go against his wishes, yet I feel that the children should have some kind of religious feelings. I just don't know how I'd go about it. I can't do too much underhand work, so I know I'd never send them to a Sunday School or a church. . . . It wouldn't be fair to John to try to instill too much religion in them. . . . I haven't decided in my own mind what I will do when my child comes and asks me who is God—a divine being or a mythical figure. This will be hard.

It is clear that not all decisions a couple are called upon to make are as ill-defined in a structural sense. For example, the man is authorized to decide in what community the couple shall reside; the female is permitted to determine questions of household management.

Because the religious question is so unstructured, if one of the partners is "victorious," he may feel somewhat uneasy about his victory. He may wonder whether he has not taken advantage of the other. A Jewish wife, whose children will be reared in her religion, commented: "I always felt that I didn't want to be one-sided about it. It worries me that this is one-sided—their being brought up Jewish—and that I am cheating my husband." By contrast, it is difficult to imagine a wife having qualms because she has taken it upon herself to make all the decisions with respect to furnishing the home.

There were four Reluctant-Amenable dyads in which no explicit decision was reached during the premarital stage.

Neither of the members committed himself to raising the children in the other's faith.* In one case, we were told that violent arguments had taken place before the marriage. The Catholic wife, who was the Reluctant member, commented:

We have not decided how to bring up our children. This is part of the terrible ethical arguments we used to have before we got married. We would both get furious and livid with rage. My husband's position is that we should wait and see what happens.

Her husband remarked, in turn:

One of my wife's great faults is that she likes to discuss these things ahead of time—that is, about the raising of the children. We discussed it somewhat before we got married, and we used to argue and disagree about this. We have not decided the issue, and we will wait until she is pregnant. No one has the moral strength to work out in advance what he will do when he is confronted with a situation. When the time comes, it is not always possible to stick to one's original plans. . . . I doubt that our children will receive any formal training.

While the other three couples were apparently not torn apart in the same manner, they, too, had formulated no specific plans. Unfortunately, we know very little about these cases. However, it appears that insofar as the partners discussed the question at all, they reached a vague understanding that any religious education their children received would be relatively mild, neither thorough nor doctrinaire. Interesting questions arise—though ones we are unable to answer—with respect to these cases: Why was the decision as to the children's religious orientation left open in these instances? Why wasn't the question resolved in favor of the Reluctant, as it was in the cases considered

* As might be expected, a civil ceremony was performed in each of these marriages.

previously? Perhaps a clue is provided by the fact that all four of the Reluctants were women and, with one exception, were older when they met their husbands than were most of the other wives interviewed. They may have been wary of making an issue of the question, at least in the pre-marital stage, for fear of driving their suitors away.

To leave our interviewees for a moment, it is interesting to speculate on the following question: When one of the partners is more attached to his heritage than the other, how frequently will the former "win out" in a "religious" struggle? If we take into account the structural setting in which the decision is reached, there would seem to be little that would militate against a victory for the more ardent member. The social structure appears to be "neutral" in this regard. To this degree, we would expect the will of the more fervent member to prevail with great regularity.

In what sense is the social structure "neutral"? For one thing, there is no higher religious authority or tribunal, to which both partners are subject, which prescribes the path to be followed when the partners adhere to different faiths. This is not to overlook the fact that each religion insists that members who outmarry should raise their offspring only within their own faith. But this, of course, provides no solution: The two partners, in effect, are urged to resolve their common problem in ways which are mutually incompatible. Since there is no court of higher appeal in the sphere of religion, the couple, as a unit, are not enjoined to follow one course rather than the other. To this extent, the more ardent member is not forced to raise the children in his partner's religion.

Second, as we suggested previously, there is no general consensus as to whether the authority to choose the child's religion properly resides with the husband or the wife. Apparently, certain cultural norms endow the male with the right to choose, while others place the prerogative in the hands of the female. As a result, the member who is more fervent, whether male or female, can appeal to those norms that invest his sex with such authority without feeling that, in so doing, he has *flagrantly* usurped the rights of the other.

Finally, it seems unlikely that the partners will have readily available much information indicating the religious course followed by other mixed couples. Facts and figures bearing upon this issue are nearly completely absent in this country. In addition, in all probability, the partners' circle of acquaintances will not include a great number of other intermarried Jews or Gentiles who were faced with, and resolved, this particular question. This is pertinent because, as is well known, the practices of others may exert considerable influence upon the decisions reached by an individual. In fact, the individual's desire to conform may even lead him to follow a path which he personally looks upon with disfavor.[3] But external guide lines are lacking with regard to the topic at hand. Accordingly, the more ardent member cannot be made to feel that his solution to the problem is atypical, and therefore untenable. His partner will not be in a position to say: "Other mixed couples don't raise their children like that! How can you even consider it?" In the absence of external guide lines, the two members must resolve this problem for themselves; and, as a result, the commanding position of the more fervent member remains unshaken.

Let us turn now to those cases where both partners were negatively predisposed toward outmarriage. In such instances, one might expect that some kind of compromise would be reached with respect to the raising of the children:

[JEWISH WIFE]: The religion of our children was the one thing we felt was a major problem for us. We certainly discussed it a lot before we were married. . . . We felt it would be easy if we stayed in New York because we could choose something like Ethical Culture or the Community Church. If we didn't stay in New York, our point of view before we married was the idealistic one: We felt if we lived in a fairly Jewish community, we would send the children to a reformed synagogue; if we lived in a Gentile community, we would try to find a good Protestant church.

In general, the Protestant husband's account was similar to his wife's:

We didn't come to any conclusion, except that in terms of religious belief the child will not be exclusively Jewish or Christian. We'll let the child know that he comes from both traditions.

That this compromise solution was not reached without some anguish on his part, however, can be inferred from his remarks below:

I don't know what our kid will do if all the others are going to Sunday School and he wants to go. I still have a lot of residual feelings. I would kind of hope that if the child identifies, it will be with a church and not a synagogue. It is part of the feeling that what I have been through is more right than what my wife has been through. Also, the child will lose status if he identifies with the Jews. I don't deny there will be problems. We say to ourselves we can't deny the child a chance to identify if others do. But I hope it is with a church and not with a synagogue.

The case that follows is of interest because, unlike the preceding one, the partners very definitely did not compromise. The Jewish wife completely prevailed over her Catholic husband and had things entirely her own way. Since it would appear that the two were about equally committed to their faiths, how can the wife's triumph be explained? Willard Waller's "principle of least interest" may provide an explanation. Waller suggests that the person who is less involved emotionally is in a position to dictate the conditions under which the affair will continue. Because he has less to lose, he can afford to make greater demands upon the other.[4] There were definite indications that the Jewish wife referred to above was less involved than her suitor. In this connection, note the remarks of the two partners as each describes how a Jewish orientation was decided upon for their children:

[JEWISH WIFE]: We always talked about what the children would be—we each wanted our own religion for them. Then he agreed to them being brought up Jewish, and shortly after that we got engaged. . . . We would have gotten married sooner except that it took Tony such a long time to decide to bring the children up Jewish, which is what I wanted. . . . This was not a difficult decision for me to make, but it was for Tony. I haven't given up anything, but he has given up his religion for the children.

[CATHOLIC HUSBAND]: [*How did you happen to decide to raise the children as Jews?*] My wife was going to have the pain and bear the children. I saw it that way. Also, I love her very much. [*Did you ever talk of bringing the children up as Catholics?*] I might have mentioned it in the beginning. But she wanted her own way, and I agreed to it. [*Did you find this an easy or difficult decision to reach?*] Not too easy—you like your way in these things. But if they're your children, you love them anyway; it's the same thing. It was not too difficult to decide. *I wanted her bad. I went along with it. You know, you just kind of go along.*

From these remarks, we can sense that the wife had more bargaining power in this situation because she was less involved. Furthermore, and in accord with ideas presented previously, we would argue that the neutrality of the social structure enabled her to make full use of this bargaining power.

Unfortunately, we have little information concerning the remaining two cases. While one of these couples was married in a civil ceremony, it is not known if a decision was reached regarding the children and, if so, what its nature may have been. The other couple was married by a rabbi, but apparently this was not viewed by either partner as necessarily foreshadowing the manner in which their children would be reared. They agreed to defer the question. The comments made by this wife, two years after her marriage, are of interest:

[JEWISH WIFE]: We haven't really made any decisions yet. In fact, we haven't talked about what religion our children will be since we were married. It seemed important before we were married, but it doesn't seem so important now. . . . Before I married, I assumed that being children of an intermarriage would be a burden for our children, because some people disapprove of anything that's different. Now I feel that if we manage to bring our children up as individuals, those people probably won't like our children or us anyway.

To summarize, we have seen that the Reluctants were anxious to have their children brought up in their faith; that their partners frequently acceded to their wishes; and that this acquiescence was one of the factors which led these relationships to eventuate in marriage. We believe that, for the most part, these concessions occurred because the two partners were not equally committed to their faiths. In one instance in which the members were equally committed, we attributed the outcome to the greater bargaining power held by the member who was less involved emotionally.

Shifting our perspective, we visualized the social structure as having contributed to the Reluctant's victory because it placed no obstacles in his path. For one thing, the mores of our society do not decree that mixed couples must follow a specified course; they are not compelled to raise their children in one religion rather than another. Furthermore, it was suggested that neither the man nor the woman is placed in a superior position in regard to this matter, that neither is granted an advantage in the struggle for religious domination. In short, whether the individual be male or female, Jew or Gentile, he has an equal opportunity, *vis à vis* his partner, of having the children raised in his faith. Assuming the above is true, there are no structural constraints to prevent Reluctants, such as those in our group, from "winning out." More specifically, there are no external factors to prevent them from having their way when they are more religious than their partners or when they are less deeply involved emotionally.

In conclusion, our discussion with regard to these matters has merely scratched the surface. Much remains to be learned about the ways in which Reluctants and their partners interact over the religious question, as well as the structural context in which the two happen to find themselves. In fact, an entire study might profitably be centered around the partners' plans for the upbringing of their children and the considerations on which their thinking is based. It is an important subject for study because the manner in which this issue is resolved may vitally affect the marital decisions of those who are negatively predisposed toward crossing ethnic lines in marriage.

The Children's Social Identity

Up to now, little heed has been paid to the fact that the Reluctant may be primarily concerned, not with his children's religious affiliation, *per se,* but with how his children will be identified socially in the eyes of others. Will his offspring be regarded as Christians and accorded the prestige of the majority? Or will they be considered Jews? Clearly, Christians who are contemplating intermarriage, even though they have few religious (or cultural) ties to their heritage, may be anxious that their offspring be looked upon as Gentiles. While the situation is not strictly analogous, Jews who are detached from their background may be intent that their children be viewed as Jewish. Resenting the invidious distinctions drawn between him and his neighbors, yet acknowledging their reality, this type of Jew may feel it would be morally wrong to detach himself from the underprivileged status assigned him. "The only thing that holds me to being Jewish," said a Jewish husband, "is that the history of the Jews is the history of persecution and I do not like persecution."

It may be that, whether he be Jewish or Gentile, typically, the Reluctant's resistance to intermarriage will stem from both religious *and* social considerations. However, it is useful to unravel these strands in order to reveal certain differences between them. Having previously considered factors bearing upon the children's religious affiliation, we shall turn now to those bearing upon their social identity.

How anxious was the Reluctant that his children bear his social identity, rather than his partner's? What were his partner's sentiments with regard to this matter? Was this an issue between them before they got married? Were they able to reach any understandings, tacit or otherwise, relating to their offspring's identification? If so, did these affect the Reluctant's decision to get married? While there is scattered evidence that the Reluctant was concerned as to how others would label his children, we know little about his and his partner's interaction with reference to this issue or the consequences such interaction might have had for his romance. Nevertheless, it is still worth considering (or, more precisely, speculating about) some of the structural aspects of this situation, because the structural context in which the Reluctant finds himself may affect what happens between him and his partner and the likelihood of his going through with the marriage.

First of all we might ask whether the social structure permits "mixed" couples to determine the social identity of their child. Can such parents see to it that their child is labeled one way rather than another? Certainly, they have some control over the matter. They can raise their youngster in a certain religion, encourage him to associate with children of a given ethnic background, live in a particular community. At the same time, these measures are no guarantee that their child will be viewed by society in accordance with their wishes. Although the youngster is a practicing Lutheran, he may be considered "really" a Jew. In short, the social identity assigned to the child will be *independent,* to some degree, of his parents' goals and the measures they may take to implement these goals. The child's social identity, unlike his religious affiliation, will be determined in part by the social structure.

At this point let us consider whether each parent wields *equal* control over the social identification of their child. To simplify matters, let us assume that both husband and wife are intent upon transmitting their own social identity to their child, but have taken no specific steps to ensure this end, such as directing his religious training. Under such conditions, what is the relative strength of each partner when the husband is Jewish and the wife is Gentile? When the husband is Gentile and the wife is Jewish? We would suggest that the likelihood that the wishes of one partner will prevail over those of the other will depend, in some measure, upon the ethnic affiliation and sex of that partner.

Looking at ethnic affiliation in isolation from all other factors, it is our guess that when the ethnic background of both parents is known, there is a greater probability that the child will be regarded as Jewish. In analogous situations, social structures reveal a tendency to relegate the "in-between" child to the lower ranking group. Thus, the offspring of Negro-white marriages are considered members of the lower caste group and assigned the status of a Negro. Similar forces may be operative with regard to children of Jewish-Gentile parentage, in that they will be labeled Jewish by society.

Toward the close of the interview, our subjects were questioned as to how they thought others would view their children. Some were completely at a loss and could venture no opinion in this connection; some felt their children would be looked upon as "mixed"; others thought their children would be considered Jewish (or Christian). However, when they had no definite religious plans for their children, those in the latter group were more likely to believe the children would be regarded as Jewish: ("Others will feel that since the children have some Jewish blood, they are Jewish." "Some people say that if a person is one sixteenth Jewish—he's Jewish.")

Interestingly, the belief that others will view their children as Jewish may induce parents to raise them as Jews (in the religious sense):

[PROTESTANT WIFE]: I believed strongly in my own faith, and the only reason I gave it up was because of society's feelings about what our children would be. I was proud of what I had—my traditions and religion. [*Why did you change?*] It was purely a practical reason. I felt I had to change because the children would be thought of as Jewish.

[PROTESTANT WIFE]: As long as we go on living so close to my husband's family, and my husband is in business with his father, I think the children should be brought up as Jewish. After all, people know that the children's father and grandfather are Jews. . . . If everyone didn't know my husband was Jewish, there might be a choice between Judaism and Christianity for our children. If only a few of our friends knew that

Carl was Jewish, I would think a lot more about what religion they should be brought up in.

Focusing upon the sex of the partners (and ignoring their ethnicity), we would expect the father to play a more decisive role in establishing the social identity of the child, judging from the fact that the patrilineal principle operates in other similar areas. The child's social identity, we strongly suspect, will be more dependent upon his father's ethnic affiliation than his mother's.

We originally raised the query as to whether one of the members of the couple had more control (in a structural sense) than the other in determining the identity of the child. In a Jewish male-Gentile female combination, we would expect that the husband would have more influence over the outcome and that the child would be more apt to be viewed as Jewish. In this instance, the husband possesses both of the attributes which are conducive to transmitting one's identity—he is a male and he is Jewish. His Gentile wife, on the other hand, possesses neither of these attributes.

We are not implying that the children born to such a couple will inevitably be viewed as Jewish. However, if such an identification is to be avoided, special steps may have to be taken. Note the remarks of a Catholic wife in this connection:

I'm hoping that our son will be thought of as Gentile, and I will do everything in my power to make it that way. If I have the money to put him through St. Mark's, St. Paul's, or Groton, he will be all right, and I won't have any trouble. But if he goes to a public school, I don't know what I'll do. . . . I don't think Richard will be thought of as Jewish, because he will be brought up in my crowd. I want him to see as little as possible of my husband's side of the family. Even now I don't like to receive them at our house. . . . I don't want Richard to know any of his Jewish cousins.

If this case involved a Jewish husband who was anxious that his son be looked upon as Jewish, would he feel it was necessary to send the boy to a Hebrew school, or that it was essential that he prevent his son from associating with members of his wife's family? It is unlikely that he would feel precautionary measures of this nature were required. In brief, we are suggesting that when the husband is a Jew and the wife a Christian, there will be more chance, other things being equal, that their children will be looked upon as Jewish.

In a Gentile husband-Jewish wife combination, which partner will have more control? Here the outcome is more unpredictable, since each of the members has one of the attributes that is conducive to passing along his identity. We are quite unprepared to say whether the husband's maleness or the wife's Jewishness is the more powerful determinant.

Finally, let us compare different types of Reluctants— Jewish men, Christian men, Jewish women, and Christian women—all of whom are anxious that their children bear their social identity. If these four types become involved with cross-ethnics, will they be equally deterred from going through with the marriage by the fear that the "wrong" identity might be assigned to their children? If these Reluctants assess the situation as we have and if we overlook variations in their partners' outlook, the barriers confronting them will not be equally imposing. Of the four types, the Jewish male's path to the altar will be the least obstructed, because he will have the best chance of transmitting his social identity. At the other extreme, the Gentile female's path will be the most obstructed, because she will have the least chance of having her children viewed as she desires.

In turn, we would expect these considerations to influence the marital decisions of each of the four types. Relatively confident that his children will bear his identity, the

Jewish male may feel less hesitant than the others about such a marriage. At the other extreme, the Christian female —fearful that her children will not bear her identity—may be the most hesitant of the four. In fact, perhaps she will *not* get married unless there are many favorable influences. For example, her partner may be particularly attractive, or he may agree unequivocally to raise the children in her faith. Whatever the role of such mitigating circumstances, the structural context in which "socially oriented" Reluctants find themselves may well affect their decisions with regard to intermarriage.

PARENTAL OPPOSITION

7 . . . *The Basis of*

Parental Opposition

UP TO THIS POINT in our study, the Reluctant's attachment
to his partner has been discussed solely in terms of their
relationship with each other. However, as mentioned earlier, the Reluctant's relationships with other people in
his environment also affected the course of his romance. In
fact, it is possible that some of these marriages would not
have taken place if these relationships had differed in certain ways. In other words, while the fact that his partner
had many compensating features, that he was willing to
subordinate his own ethnic ties to those of the Reluctant,
etc., were of major importance in bringing about the marriage, these were not the only influences present. Throughout the remainder of this study, attention will be focused
upon the Reluctant's relationships with his parents and
friends in order to determine how these factors affected the
course of his romance.

With only a few exceptions, the Reluctants' parents were
opposed to the marriage, and many were bitterly opposed.
Furthermore, their feelings were not a matter of indifference to their children. The Reluctants in our group had

cared a good deal about their parents' reactions; in fact, it was because of this parental disapproval—or the prospect of it—that many of our subjects were so antagonistic toward intermarriage. We might well wonder then why these parents were not able to prevail over their children, that is, why they were unable to forestall the relationship or put an end to it, once it had developed. Phrased another way, what enabled these romances to develop within settings which were so hostile to their very existence?

In the present section we shall deal primarily with this general question. First, however, we will provide an over-all picture of the oppositional forces which confronted our subjects, in order to give the reader a picture of what they were actually up against, so to speak. Accordingly, in this chapter we shall discuss the reasons for parental opposition; in the next chapter we shall describe parental efforts to break up the relationship. We shall then return to our original concern: How were these romances able to develop in the face of the forces arrayed against them?

In this phase of our investigation, we have included, along with the Reluctants, about twenty-five cases in which the respondent was categorized as an Amenable. These Amenables were not averse to outmarrying in an over-all sense; however, this does not mean the opposition of their parents did not deter them to some extent. Our evidence suggests that the opposition of their parents was indeed a deterring element, although, in general, parental disapproval seemed to be of lesser concern to them than to the Reluctants.* In other words, if we consider only the parent-

---

* That these Amenables were not indifferent to their parents' feelings is suggested by the way they rated themselves on a five-point scale when asked: "How close were you to your parents when you were growing up?" Their answers were as follows: very close 3; close 11; moderate 7; not particularly close 2; not at all close 1.

It should be pointed out that, in several instances, the prospect of parental disapproval, instead of acting as a deterrent, apparently led the Amenable to seek out cross-ethnics and promoted the relationship once it

child relationship—apart from everything else—the relationship between the opposed parents and the Reluctant bears enough similarity to the relationship between the opposed parents and the Amenable to warrant including the latter subjects in this discussion.

Why were these parents so opposed to intermarriage? Our subjects mentioned many reasons, which can be grouped as follows: Their parents were opposed for "basic" reasons; or because they anticipated the marriage would give rise to certain problems; or because they were sensitive to the opinions of others.* While these groupings are arbitrary, they are useful for our purposes.

First, let us turn to some of the "basic" reasons Jewish parents were opposed to intermarriage. Aside from jeopardizing the cultural identity of their sons or daughters, intermarriage was considered morally "wrong":

---

was under way. For example, a Jewish husband told us that, in contemplating his marriage, he had experienced a "subtle and enjoyable feeling of irking his mother." If we focus a moment upon children who wish to punish their parents, intermarriage would seem to be a particularly suitable way of accomplishing this end. Not only is it a "disgraceful" act, *per se,* but it is exceedingly *visible* to other persons, such as relatives and friends of the family. Among such rebellious acts we might also include: bearing an illegitimate child, being apprehended as a delinquent, and failing to progress in school. None of these "misbehaviors" escapes the notice of others. In addition, insofar as they are retaliatory measures, such acts would seem to be even more appropriate today than they were in former years. Formerly, such acts were ascribed more readily to inherent defects in the child himself, to shortcomings in his "character" or "constitution." Today, because of a shift in the psychological climate of opinion, parents are held increasingly *responsible* for the conduct of their offspring. If their child outmarries, for example, parents may be held accountable for this, both by others and by themselves. (A Catholic husband in our group remarked: "My parents aren't over it yet. Mother feels she is a failure because I intermarried and will have nothing to do with the church.")

* Here, as elsewhere in this section, we have had to rely on the respondent's version of his parents' feelings, outlook, and behavior. It goes without saying that if we had interviewed the parents themselves, we would have obtained more detailed and more accurate information.

[JEWISH DAUGHTER]: My mother was very upset about it. And so was my father. They equated it with a kind of moral transgression, as though I were going out with a married man or having an illegitimate child. . . . They felt it was a disgrace for a Jew to marry a Gentile—it just *is,* and they didn't give any reasons. They said things like they were glad their parents were dead, rather than have them know what I was doing. They never said that I couldn't be happy with him, but it was just morally wrong.

[JEWISH SON]: [*What was it about her being Gentile that they objected to?*] There were social and family reasons. . . . The whole idea that one should marry within his group was very deeply ingrained in them. They just believed it all their lives. It is the same as asking us—why do you feel that it's wrong to rob a bank?

In one instance, it was even suggested that the marriage might have supernatural repercussions: "My wife's mother [Jewish] had had cancer, and she felt that God had helped her to overcome it. She felt the Jewish God should not be scorned by an intermarriage."

In addition, some Jewish parents were concerned because, to their way of thinking, all Gentiles were hostile to Jews:

[JEWISH DAUGHTER]: My mother feels all Gentiles are anti-Semitic. Her parents were killed in a pogrom and people in their town . . . who were "friends" of theirs participated.

[JEWISH SON]: My parents felt that all Gentiles hated Jews. This was a result of their whole education. They never got over that.

[JEWISH SON]: My mother had the feeling that one can trust one of one's own faith better. She was not against it on principle—it was just a matter of playing it safe.

The Christian parents, too, were distressed because of the religious and/or cultural implications of such a marriage:

[PROTESTANT SON]: The basis of my mother's opposition was religious. I would be lost if I married outside my religion. . . . She regarded my marrying a Jewish person as not taking religion seriously. To her, her religion was the only correct one.

[CATHOLIC SON]: Mother wept. She was upset because I wasn't marrying a Catholic girl. She was upset because there would not be a church ceremony with all its significance. The greatest shock of all was that my parents had to come to grips with reality: I wasn't still a Catholic.

In other instances, social considerations apparently played a major role:

[PROTESTANT DAUGHTER]: My mother said, "You have an old family and a fine one. You should marry someone of equally good family—don't taint the blood! Governor————was an ancestor of yours!"

[JEWISH DAUGHTER-IN-LAW]: My in-laws objected because they hated Jews. They were real anti-Semites, from way back. My husband's friends were never welcome in the house, and I was never in the house when my in-laws were there until after we were married.

In looking ahead to the future, these parents (whatever their religion) saw the marriage as giving rise to a variety of problems. First of all, many felt such a marriage had little chance of success: ("They were concerned that it would not work out, and that I would be unhappy." "They thought that it would mean that we would never get along and fight a lot." "They felt it would break up.") A Jewish daughter recalled her mother's prophecy: "When you and your husband argue after you are married, he'll be sure to denounce you as a Jew—in his heart he probably hates Jews." Some parents believed the difference in religious beliefs, aside from creating a schism between the partners, would lead to other personal difficulties. "My mother didn't really believe I was an agnostic," remarked a Protestant daughter. "She felt that I would get more religious as I got older, and that this would be a problem."

The children's relationship with their prospective in-laws constituted another problem area. The parents felt their offspring would be harshly received. A Catholic wife recalled her mother's warning: "His family will never accept you. What kind of life will that be?" In another instance, the parents predicted that members of the other family would "gang up" on their child; in a third case, that the in-laws would attempt to break up the marriage:

[JEWISH DAUGHTER]: My husband's parents were born in Italy, and my mother felt they were backward. From what she had seen and heard, she was sure they would try to break up the marriage. She told me I shouldn't have a baby right away, so I wouldn't get stuck with him if his parents tried to break it up.

Another Jewish daughter expressed herself similarly:

My father was against it because, as a cop, he saw only the rough side of life. On the lower east side where he worked, there were few Jews and mostly Italians and Irish. The Italians and Irish caused all the trouble there, and he didn't want any part of it.

Generally speaking, parents are probably aware that their child's marriage will weaken the affective ties between them, no matter who the partner. But these bonds may become even more tenuous if the partner's background and way of life is "alien." In a sense, a stranger—and one to whom they are not favorably disposed—has thrust himself between them and their children and, in the process, may completely destroy the close ties which existed previously.[1] A marriage of this type may constitute a serious threat to parents. In explaining his parents' opposition, a Jewish son said, "They were afraid they might lose me from the family." And a Catholic son, whose parents balked at the prospect of his being married by a rabbi, commented: "This was an indication to them of my first step toward Judaism. They felt this whole thing would create a gap between myself and them." Here, parental worries centered on their own relationship with their children in the future.

Finally, and as might be expected, parents were concerned about the fate of their grandchildren:

[JEWISH SON]: They were afraid that I would lose my identity as a Jew and that the children would be bastardized.

[CATHOLIC DAUGHTER]: My mother said you must have some sort of religion, and your children must, too. But not Jewish for your children—she could never see any of our children being Jewish!

[CATHOLIC DAUGHTER]: My mother was horrified at his being Jewish. . . . The children would not have the advantages I had had. . . . She felt they might be born with Jewish features or revert back to their Jewish ancestry.

To review, the opposition of these parents stemmed from basic convictions of theirs (e.g., that intermarriage was morally "wrong") and, in addition, reflected the fact that certain problems were anticipated if the marriage took place. However, there were other reasons for parental opposition as well. The disapproval of others was frequently looked upon by our respondents as being an important, and occasionally the most important, determinant of their parents' opposition:

[JEWISH SON]: My mother's qualms were not due so much to her own misgivings; it was a matter of saving face . . . before friends and relatives. She told me the relatives had questioned her and she was uncomfortable.

[CATHOLIC DAUGHTER-IN-LAW]: The reasons they gave me for objecting were that they couldn't face their friends and relatives if this terrible thing happened. They said they'd rather see their son dead.

[CATHOLIC DAUGHTER]: My parents said, "If he didn't look so Jewish, it wouldn't be so bad! What will our friends and neighbors think?"

We cannot know whether these particular parents were actually as sensitive to outside opinion as their children (or their children's partners) made them out to be. But if they were, their sensitivity may have stemmed from a belief that others would hold them accountable for this "terrible thing." In the contemporary scene, parents are believed to play a very important role in the formation of their children's personalities. Should their offspring later "misbehave," the responsibility for this transgression is apt to be placed squarely at the feet of the parents. In other words, while the parents in our group were, understandably, distressed because their children were contemplating an act condemned by friends and relatives, their distress may have been increased by the fear that others would view them— not their children—as ultimately responsible.*

Before we conclude this phase of our discussion, let us look at a few instances in which there was no opposition to the marriage, although it would have developed under

* Perhaps this explains why relatives were, seemingly, more ready to forgive: ("My very orthodox grandmother . . . cried because she didn't want me to marry Gus, but afterward she was the first one to come around and persuade the others it was going to be all right.") Since relatives probably felt they would not be held accountable for the marriage, they may have been more willing to accept it.

other conditions. A Jewish mother thought highly of her daughter's Gentile suitor and felt he was "nicer" than her other boy friends, who were Jewish:

[JEWISH DAUGHTER]: My mother would have been happier if Bob had been Jewish, but she thought he was much nicer than any of the Jewish boys I had gone with. I thought my grandmother was going to object a lot—she's so religious. I was afraid she would haunt my mother about the whole thing until she collapsed. But I was surprised: my gra̶n̶d̶ ̶ ̶ ̶ ̶er liked him from the sta̶r̶t̶ ̶ey all liked ̶ ̶n they had ̶ ̶car. If my ̶ ̶ngs for her. ̶ ̶ged to be- ̶ ̶own way. ̶ ̶he candles ̶ ̶of thing.

̶ ̶laughter, ̶ ̶ere were ̶ ̶n really ̶ ̶r could ̶ ̶made a ̶ ̶of her

My parents met him early in our courtship. In the latter part of June, he came to the house for the first time to take me out. My parents liked him when they met him and did nothing to discourage me from seeing him and getting serious about him. [*How did they feel about his being Jewish?*] They didn't say anything. *This was the first time I had expressed any serious interest in anyone.* They were delighted to see they were getting rid of me. [*What did they like about him particularly?*] They thought he was agreeable, likable, friendly, considerate, and it was apparent that he was fond of me. They thought that he would make me happy. *He was a physician, and this meant security, and they liked that.* They wouldn't have accepted his being Jewish so graciously if he had been a ditch digger.

Finally, a Jewish mother was disturbed that her son was still unmarried at thirty, plus the fact that her own illness prevented her from taking care of him:

[JEWISH SON]: When I was going with a Gentile before the service, my mother had a fit. She was glad I ceased and desisted. When I got out of service, she wanted me to get married. She was very anxious about it. Slowly but surely all my friends were getting married, and it annoyed her no end. First I told her I was going with a girl, and then I told her she was non-Jewish. Surprisingly, she wasn't shocked or upset. I think there were two reasons for this. First of all, she was confined to the hospital and was very ill. She was unhappy about this situation both for herself and for me. Aside from this, she was anxious for me to get married, anxious for someone to take care of me.

8 . . . *Parental Efforts*
to Deal with
the Relationship

PREVIOUSLY, we considered the reasons why parents were opposed to the marriage. Let us now examine how they handled the situation which confronted them.

First of all, it should be noted that the parents' behavior (and feelings) underwent changes as the courtship progressed. At the stage when they believed the couple were only casually acquainted, they were not greatly alarmed. At this point, they merely protested—and sometimes quite mildly—but did not actively intervene:

[JEWISH DAUGHTER]: My mother was a little against my going out with so many Gentile boys, but she never got too upset about it because she figured I was not serious about any of them and just going out didn't mean anything.

[JEWISH SON]: At first they were not excited, because they did not think anything was imminent. After we told them about our marriage plans, there was quite a to-do and a prolonged one. My mother was very upset.

[JEWISH SON]: At first they were mildly displeased, but not enough so that you could notice it. Later on, they hit the ceiling. They tried their best to talk me out of it.

Like some of the Reluctants discussed earlier, these parents thought nothing serious would develop: ("They didn't make an issue of the romance because they thought it would blow over.") On the whole, we know little about why they were so certain the affair would remain "innocent." In one instance, the parents felt that the fact that their son was going overseas in the army would put an end to the affair. In other instances, their children's youth was a source of reassurance:

[CATHOLIC DAUGHTER]: When I first started dating Robert, my mother had no particular feelings. She thought he was a nice fellow, and since we were both just in high school, she didn't take it too seriously.

However, their conviction that the relationship "wouldn't amount to anything" did not necessarily mean that these parents were unconcerned about what was going on, or that their protests were always mild. In several instances, the parents were immediately outraged. They did not want their children to associate with members of the other ethnic group even under the most casual circumstances.

We were interested in the way these parents behaved toward their children when they realized that their relationship with their partner was more than a casual one, when they foresaw the possibility of a marriage.* For one thing, they verbalized—or continued to verbalize—the reasons they felt such a marriage should most certainly be

* We will consider the parent-partner relationship at a later point.

avoided: It was morally reprehensible; it would lead to innumerable problems, etc. Whatever the effect of these arguments, they did not seriously influence the course of the romance. As a result, these parents brought additional pressures to bear.

However, there were several cases where, once they had voiced their objections, parents attempted to exert little, if any, further influence:

[CATHOLIC DAUGHTER]: My father stated his opposition as an indication of how he felt, not as an order to me. He said, after all, it was my final choice. . . . My parents never tried to influence me directly. Of course, my mother found lots of men around home for me to go out with, but there were no orders given.

[PROTESTANT DAUGHTER]: They were really rather upset, but didn't want to show it. . . . They didn't try to influence me. In fact, we didn't discuss it much, and they were reticent about bringing up the whole subject. The only argument they used was that we were so very different in our backgrounds.

Presumably, the restraint exercised by these parents was a reflection of our cultural norms governing the selection of a mate: The choice must be left to the individual, and others (in this case, parents) should not attempt to influence his decision. While these norms did not succeed in silencing or immobilizing many of the parents in our group, they did keep parents from intervening as freely and as frequently as they might have in another cultural setting. For example, our subjects were asked to compare (on a five-point scale) the opposition felt and the opposition expressed by their parents when they first learned the romance was serious; it turned out that sixteen out of fifty felt their parents had expressed less opposition than they actually felt.

Nevertheless, the parents in our group were a long way

from relinquishing all further attempts to put an end to the affair. After they found that their verbal objections were of little avail, they tried to separate the couple in a variety of other ways:

1. On occasion, they tried to prevent the partners from meeting in the future: Several daughters were flatly forbidden to see their suitors again. Other parents apparently felt it would be safer if more physical distance were placed between the pair. "As soon as they knew I was serious," declared a Protestant daughter, "they tried to send me off to Japan, where my sister lived. When that didn't work, they tried to get me to go to Europe. . . ."

2. Clearly, parents cannot commandeer the emotions of their children any more than army directives can force enlisted men to feel respect for their officers. However, by manipulating certain aspects of the courtship, parents may hope to create a set of conditions which will lead their children to become "disenchanted":

[JEWISH DAUGHTER]: One of their "solutions" was postponing our marriage until we had $10,000 in the bank. The idea was that it would take us such a long time that one of us would change our mind.

[CATHOLIC DAUGHTER]: My mother insisted David come to the apartment every night, and then she went out and left us together for four or five hours, thinking we would get sick of each other if we had to see each other so often.

At a later point, her family counted on the likelihood that the couple would be ostracized by their friends:

My uncle was the one who persuaded Mother to allow us to be engaged, in the hope that it would break us up eventually. I believe my uncle thought that we would find out that no one

would associate with us during the engagement period and this
would end our relationship.

In another instance, a Protestant mother encouraged her
daughter to see more of Jews in general in the hope that
she would become disillusioned by what she saw and break
off her own romance:

[PROTESTANT DAUGHTER]: My husband couldn't get a vacation
when we planned to get married, so we thought we would go
to Florida together in January and have our good time and our
honeymoon before we were married. My mother thought this
was a good idea, because she said we would get to know each
other so much better. [*Didn't she object to your going off with
him alone?*] She thought that we would get to know each
other and maybe call the whole thing off. A doctor in town
had said to her, "Wait till your daughter sees the Jews at their
resorts! She'll be so disgused that the whole thing will be
finished." My mother felt that if we went there together, and
I saw what kind of people were there that I would call it all off.

3. In more than a few instances, the parents' impression
of the partner, as it was related to their son or daughter,
was far from flattering:

[JEWISH SON]: When my parents met my wife they took a personal dislike to her. They said nasty things about her. . . . They
said she was ugly, they said they couldn't understand anything
she said, they found her ill-bred. . . .

[JEWISH DAUGHTER]: My mother said how dreadful he was, and
how being a psychologist was no way to make a living.

One cannot help but wonder about such "images." Did
they reflect these parents' honest opinions, the opinions
they held in private? On the contrary, we believe, in the
first place, that these "images" may have served as a screen
for other objections. Quite possibly, these parents felt it

would be "wrong," or at least inexpedient, to make too
great an issue of the partner's ethnic affiliation. After all,
such objections are hardly consistent with democratic principles. As a result, they may have been looking for a more
"legitimate" way to express their disapproval. The following excerpts are revealing in this connection:

[JEWISH SON]: My parents tried to talk me out of it. They said,
"The problem is too great; how can you do this thing!" They
said that my wife had dirty fingernails, that she was too sophisticated. They criticized her for everything except the fact that she
was Gentile. Her being Gentile was the underlying reason they
were against her. [*Why do you think they didn't mention this?*]
My parents were all for the great American ideal of democracy,
for the ideal that there is no difference between groups. They
could not freely admit that their feelings were prejudiced.

[CATHOLIC DAUGHTER]: My mother had a number of excuses for
how she felt, and they all came down to his being Jewish. They
were—he walks with a limp. Then when we wanted to wait to
get married because we didn't have any money, she said, "What
kind of a fellow is he with no money and he wants to get
married! He has nothing for himself!"

Aside from expressing their disapproval in ways which
they felt were more "proper," these parents may have been
expressing *more* disapproval, in an over-all sense, than they
actually felt. In other words, the impression they expressed
of the partner as a total person may have been more negative than the opinion they held privately. Perhaps these
parents felt their children would be more likely to put an
end to the relationship if they "understood" just how odious
the partner was in their eyes:

[JEWISH SON]: My mother was quite excited. She said that I
should call it off, she did everything to see that I would call it
off. She said that Jane was older than I was, she said that Jane
was not pretty. *My mother did everything to tear her down.*

[JEWISH DAUGHTER]: My mother and I had long arguments. . . .
She tried every way she knew to talk me out of it—*but mostly
by tearing him down as a person.*

We might speculate as to when parents, in general,
would be most likely to use such "depreciating tactics."
Perhaps they will employ such tactics when they do not
have access to other forms of control and as a result must
rely more heavily on those at their disposal. To illustrate,
when a child is older, parents have fewer ways of dis-
couraging him from seeing a particular member of the opposite sex: They cannot "forbid" him to see this person;
nor can they invoke various punishments and threats. Lacking these techniques, but anxious to deter him, they may
rely more heavily upon depreciating his partner's worth.

To consider this matter further, parents have fewer
means available to them for controlling the romantic attachments of their sons than of their daughters. Traditionally, the male is more independent. When he becomes an
adult, the chances are that he will be financially self-suffi-
cient and live away from home.[1] Accordingly, if his parents
wish to discourage one of his attachments, quite possibly
they will malign his girl friend, since other techniques, for
the most part, are denied them. From this it would follow
that, other things being equal, a potential daughter-in-law,
rather than a son-in-law, would be more apt to be maligned
by parents.*

4. In the techniques described so far, the parents focused
their disruptive efforts on the partners. However, some of
the parents in our group tried to end the relationship by
arousing feelings of shame and remorse in their children,
by appealing to their sense of filial obligation:

* In this connection, it is interesting to take note of a finding from
another study—namely, that after the marriage, parents more frequently
find fault with a daughter-in-law than a son-in-law.[2] Perhaps this is, in
part, a carry-over of premarital response patterns.

[JEWISH SON]: My mother said it was making her sick, that it was killing her, and that I did not care for her. It was mostly a kind of bludgeoning. They said I should do something for my parents.

[PROTESTANT SON]: Mother emphasized the sacrifices she had made in bringing me up—you might summarize it under the words: I was ungrateful. She said my father was too deeply hurt to even speak about it. She talked about the pain involved. After the theme of sacrifice, she said I was making them a laughing stock and that I was turning my back on the religion that they had taken such pains to instill in me. There were endless variations on these themes.

[PROTESTANT DAUGHTER]: My mother's technique was to shame me. . . . She did this with tears and a general air of sadness. When I'd come into the living room and say something to her, she'd burst into tears and run out.

5. Aggressive feelings were sometimes expressed more directly. "When my mother found out," a Jewish son stated, "she said she would throw me out of the house—to never come around again." And a Catholic son remarked: "With my father it was very, very bad. He threatened to lock me out a couple of times." Another mother punished her daughter by converting a pleasant relationship into a miserable one:

[CATHOLIC DAUGHTER]: My mother threatened me in a way by refusing to talk to me. When you live with another person, and you've always been close to them, that can really make life miserable. Not even a hello when you come home, and never saying a word to you.

Occasionally, our subjects were confronted with threats of what *would* happen if the relationship eventuated in marriage. A Catholic daughter exclaimed, "They threatened to cut me off with no allowance, no inheritance, no money at all!" And five Jewish children were warned that the marriage would mean the end of their relationship with their parents: ("My parents made it clear that if I persisted, they would disown me." "They threatened never to associate with me again, and said they'd never forget or forgive what I had done." "They said they would never walk into our house after we were married.")

6. Finally, some parents hoped that "outsiders" might be able to bring their children to their "senses":

[JEWISH SON]: My parents called up my best friend and tried to get him to prevail over me.

[PROTESTANT DAUGHTER]: I was away from home at the time at college. My parents enlisted the aid of my favorite teacher. He was quite fond of me. His talking to me cut a lot of ice with me. . . . My parents wrote a lot of letters and had the whole shebang out against me—all the way up to the psychiatrist and the Dean.

[CATHOLIC DAUGHTER]: Uncle George is my mother's brother, and they always run to each other when they have troubles. She ran to him when we got serious about each other . . . and told him her troubles. She hoped he would talk me out of it.

[JEWISH SON]: My mother has a brother—he's a doctor and has high standing in our family. His word is respected on all things —on athletics, politics, and so forth. Such people are looked up to in the Jewish community. There was no pacifying my folks until I agreed to talk to my uncle. To make the situation clearer —you see, when my mother learned about this thing, she was hysterical. She asked me to see my uncle, and I certainly couldn't say no at the moment. I saw him, and he was very opposed to it. He cited chapter and verse about how some of his friends had made mixed marriages, and that they were all unsuccessful and that they were all unhappy today. He was of the opinion that I was mentally maladjusted.

In conclusion, it should be recognized that the subjects' parents did not necessarily confine themselves to any one tactic. Sometimes they used a number of them simultaneously; and as the courtship moved ahead, sometimes they abandoned certain tactics and adopted others.

During the interviewing, we were also concerned with the parents' conduct *vis à vis* the partners. Did they verbalize their feelings or make their attitudes plain in other ways? Apart from these techniques, did they employ other forms of pressure, such as those which were brought to bear upon their children?

Regarding the second question, on the whole, other forms of pressure were not brought to bear. If for no other reason, parents are largely denied the opportunity to pressure the children of others in the manner in which they can pressure their own. They cannot capitalize upon a close emotional relationship; they cannot appeal to a sense of filial obligation; nor are they in a position to invoke other punishments or threats. Perhaps this explains why a few of these parents went directly to the parents on the other side, hoping that *they* would exert pressure upon the "culprit." In other words, their relative helplessness may have led them to seek out those who were in a position to alter the chain of events. Here again, it would appear, they were "enlisting the aid of others."

To return to our first question as to whether these parents let the partner know how they felt, in about half of our cases, they expressed their feelings in whole or in part. What is perhaps most noteworthy is the manner in which these sentiments were conveyed. Rather than directly confronting the partner and verbalizing their feelings, they tended to convey them in a more indirect manner:

[CATHOLIC SON-IN-LAW]: Her parents were cold to me. Whenever I called for her, they never showed themselves, they never asked me in. Her mother used to look right past me.

[JEWISH SON-IN-LAW]: When I met my wife's mother, she immediately went to the telephone and called her husband. She said, "It's true—he's Jewish!" They were polite, but distant. Her mother strongly advised me not to marry her daughter— she said there was insanity in the family. She said, "It would be nice to see you now and then." She was implying that I should pay a visit now and then since I would not be part of the family.

[PROTESTANT DAUGHTER-IN-LAW]: The first time they ever had matzos in the house was when I came to visit, and they ostentatiously had them on the table.

[PROTESTANT DAUGHTER]: The first time my future husband came to the house, my parents didn't know he was Jewish until after he left. The second time he came, my father—knowing he was Jewish—wouldn't eat at the same table. When Bill came in and sat down, my father got up and left the room and wouldn't speak to him.*

Although they did not express their feelings directly, the parents described above undoubtedly made these feelings clear. However, seemingly, about half the parents in our group did not even try to convey their distress in an indirect manner:

[JEWISH SON-IN-LAW]: I knew my wife's mother objected because I was a Jew, but I never knew how violently. When I met her, she was a perfect lady. She never conveyed a feeling of dislike.

[PROTESTANT DAUGHTER-IN-LAW]: My husband's mother was always nice to me, and her feelings never came out into the open.

Before we proceed, let us reflect on some of the possible consequences of a situation where parents who are opposed

---

* The way these parents expressed themselves leads one to wonder why negative feelings and opinions are expressed indirectly in some face-to-face situations, while in others they are expressed directly.[3] What are the psychological and sociological conditions responsible for the same sentiment being communicated in a different fashion?

to a marriage contemplated by their children do not disclose their feelings to the partner. For one thing, this situation may lead the partner to be unaware of, or to underestimate their disapproval. The findings of another study[4] are relevant in this connection. A group of 425 divorced women were asked the following question: "Would you try to tell me, in general, what your family and your husband's family thought about your marriage several years ago, when you were beginning this marriage?" Whereas 40 per cent of these women reported that their own family had disapproved of the marriage, only 25 per cent said their husband's family had disapproved. In interpreting these results, the author writes, "It seems safe to say that this difference expresses not so much an *objective* difference in attitude on the part of these circles as it does a difference in the perception or knowledge of the respondent. The difference is a function of the *wife* reporting. That is to say, she actually *knew* the disapproving attitudes of her own family . . . while she guessed or supposed that her husband's family . . . felt approval unless she had the contrary evidence."[5] In line with our previous remarks, the lack of awareness of these women probably stemmed, in part, from a tendency on the part of their in-laws to withhold any negative feelings.

Moreover, we would suspect that, among these subjects, the woman's failure to recognize her prospective in-laws' opposition prior to the marriage served to facilitate the marriage. In this connection, the following case, among others in our group, is revealing. A Jewish wife indicated that her mother had been "strongly against the whole thing." However, when her husband was asked if his wife's mother had been opposed to their marriage, he answered: "Not from what I understand. . . . Well, probably she would have liked her daughter to marry a Jewish boy, but she liked me. . . . They took it as it came." And, significantly, he added, "Their attitude made things a lot easier."

To pursue this matter further, the tendency of prospective in-laws to curb their feelings may be especially significant for the Christian member of a Jewish-Gentile couple. The non-Jewish member may not be aware of how strongly Jews feel about intermarriage.

[PROTESTANT WIFE]: Before I met my husband, I didn't feel hesitant about marrying a Jew. Ignorance is bliss. I didn't know what I was getting into. I figured marrying a Jew would make about as much difference as when a Baptist marries a Methodist. Even though I minored in religion at college, I didn't realize the Jewish people felt so strongly about intermarriage.

If his prospective Jewish in-laws are opposed to the marriage and if they disclose their feelings, their unfavorable reactions may come as a shock to the Christian partner, and the relationship may receive quite a jolt:

[CATHOLIC WIFE]: I learned about their feelings a month before we were to get married. Five months before they had come to our engagement party, so I was really shocked and upset when all these feelings came out. . . . I gave him back his ring and told him I didn't want to fight his mother.

[PROTESTANT WIFE]: I did not feel hesitant about becoming involved with Arthur at first, but then later I did when there was this hue and cry from his family. I was upset, because they weren't going to come to the wedding—so we called the whole thing off and decided not to get married. This was a very trying situation. . . . I felt it would be too difficult with his parents.

On the other hand, if the partner is Jewish, he will be more apt to suspect his prospective in-laws are resistant to intermarriage. A Protestant girl said, "I didn't expect this tremendous block on the part of my mother when it came to my marrying a Jew. . . . *My husband* was not half so surprised at my mother's reactions." If there is parental opposition and if it is revealed to the Jewish member, the latter's suspicions will only be confirmed. Because the news is not a shattering surprise, as it may well be for the Christian, the romance will probably suffer a lesser blow.

It was suggested previously that when in-laws do not reveal their disapproval, the partner may fail to recognize its presence and that this will expedite the marriage. However, this is not to imply that the partner's assessment of the situation will be wholly dependent upon his in-laws' overt reactions. Obviously, there are other ways in which he may learn of their feelings, apart from personal observation. A few of these "other ways" were described by our interviewees.

A Jewish wife revealed that the anti-Semitism of her future in-laws was "common knowledge":

I assumed they were violently opposed because I knew from the beginning that they hated Jews. . . . I didn't learn about it directly from them because I never spoke to them or met them until a few months after we were married. It was common knowledge around the neighborhood how they felt.

In one case the partner was "alerted" by his friends:

[CATHOLIC SON-IN-LAW]: Most of the crowd [*they were all Jewish*] found out before I did that her father objected to me. I was the last one to know. . . . The others [*aside from a close friend*] did not have the heart to say anything. It was like telling a friend he has B.O. . . . My friend opened up the situation to me. He said, "Jack, her mother and father don't like you." He couldn't explain it, so I asked my wife about it. She said that I wasn't Jewish, and her father didn't like the idea of her going out with a Gentile.

However, the chief source of the partner's information regarding his in-law's disapproval (when it was not directly disclosed) was his future mate. Of course, this is hardly surprising, for when a man and woman have established an intimate relationship, they are certainly prone to reveal

what is on their minds. The pressing concerns of one partner are not apt to remain hidden from the other: A Catholic wife recalled, "We went out together the day after I
met his parents, and my husband was very quiet. I could
see something was troubling him. So I asked him, and he
told me that even though his folks liked me very much,
they were very upset about it."

Apart from the fact that intimacy leads to "openness,"
there were additional reasons why our subjects divulged
their parents' feelings. On several occasions, the knowledge
that their *partners'* parents were opposed to their relationship prompted them to disclose the disapproval of their
own parents:

[PROTESTANT WIFE]: My husband was very tight-lipped about
his family and how they felt. . . . I don't remember him saying
anything, but he must have at one time said something like,
"Well, don't think *my* family is overjoyed about this!"

In another case, a Jewish wife, who was intent that her
religious demands be met, was "very frank" in disclosing
her mother's feelings. Perhaps she believed that if she
warned her boy friend of the strength of the forces pitted
against him, he would be more likely to yield to her wishes.
On other occasions, the partners revealed this information
to their future mates shortly before they were to meet their
parents for the first time. Understandably, they wanted to
forewarn their partners, to prepare them for what might
well be an unfriendly reception.

Finally, it bears repeating that our subjects were not always aware of their prospective in-laws' opposition. In
some instances, neither the in-laws, nor their children, nor
outsiders transmitted this information. Apart from the fact
that this sometimes expedited the marriage, it had other
effects as well. To illustrate, a Protestant wife, who had
been married for four years, remarked:

My husband [still] doesn't know anything about it [*i.e., parental disapproval during the courtship*]. I've never said much about it. I knew what I was going to do. . . . We all have to live happily together. My mother's come to love him. I would much rather have no friction.

We might say that this woman acted as a "buffer." She insulated her partner from the reality of the situation, in the hope (which was apparently realized) that this would lead to more harmonious post-marital relationships.

To summarize this chapter, we dwelt, first, upon the parent-child relationship and enumerated the ways in which parents brought pressure to bear upon their children in an effort to prevent their marriage. We then shifted our attention to the relationship between in-law and partner and noted that, in conveying their feelings, in-laws tended to do so in an indirect manner, and that frequently they chose not to reveal their feelings at all. The self-restraint of in-laws (when the partner was not otherwise informed of their feelings) was looked upon as facilitating several of the romances.

Finally, if we compare the behavior of parents toward their children with their behavior toward the children's partners, it is apparent that their efforts to sever the relationship centered on the former. It was the children, not their partners, who bore the brunt of the parents' attack.

9 . . . *The Ineffectiveness of*

Parental Opposition

IN THE FOREGOING chapters, we depicted the oppositional forces which confronted the young people in our group. On the basis of the data we collected, it is apparent that their parents did not merely question the advisability of their marriage or suggest that the decision be considered carefully. They were intent on putting an end to the relationship and, with this objective in mind, brought considerable pressure to bear.

When we recall that many of our subjects had maintained close ties with their parents and that few were totally indifferent or estranged, we might wonder how these romances ever managed to develop at all. In other words, if we had not known the results of these romances beforehand, we would not have been surprised to find that parental opposition had prevented half of these marriages. But, of course, these couples did get married, and the question arises as to how this came about. More specifically, were any factors operating which lessened the effectiveness of parental opposition?

The Perceptual Lag of Parents

As we have seen, the manner in which the parents reacted to the romance was dependent, by and large, upon how serious they believed it to be. The more serious it appeared, the more distraught they became—and the more pressure they brought to bear. In view of this, the following question arises: What was the relationship between the parents' image of the romance on the one hand and the actual status of the romance on the other? Were the parents aware of the feelings the partners entertained for each other at the time the partners were experiencing these feelings? In the group we studied, the parents' image of what was happening lagged behind the actual course of events, and this, in turn, had certain consequences for the courtships with which we are concerned.

In the course of the interview, each respondent was asked how aware his parents had been of the existence of his relationship with his future mate. Did they know about it from the beginning? If they did, were they aware of its continued development at the time such development occurred? Of the sets of parents who had been opposed to the relationship, over 80 per cent were either unaware of its existence initially and/or failed to keep abreast of its future development. In other words, only a minority had an accurate picture of the relationship from beginning to end. With regard to the parents who had not been opposed, one out of two had an accurate picture of the entire affair. In short, those parents who were opposed to the romance perceived it inaccurately, in that their view of the status of the relationship lagged behind the actual course of events.

Before turning to these "non-aware" parents, it should be noted that several sets of parents apparently knew what was going on, but did not know that their future in-law

was a member of the outgroup. On occasion, they were
kept in the dark for only a brief period; at other times, they
remained ignorant of the true situation throughout most—
or all—of the affair:

[CATHOLIC DAUGHTER-IN-LAW]: I met my husband's folks, and
they liked me. Then, because his folks liked me right off, Godfrey felt they might take it better than he had figured at first,
so he casually let it drop once that I was not Jewish. . . .

[CATHOLIC SON]: For the first two years that I went with my
wife, my mother did not know she was Jewish.

[CATHOLIC DAUGHTER-IN-LAW]: My husband's mother didn't
know for a long time that I wasn't Jewish. He introduced me as
Jewish, and she didn't know until the night before the wedding,
when one of my sisters called her up and told her.

Let us now turn to those parents who, as far as we know,
were never under such misapprehensions. Some parents in
this group knew nothing, or practically nothing, about the
romance in its early phase; however, they became fully informed at a later point:

[JEWISH DAUGHTER]: My parents didn't know from the beginning that Leonard and I were seeing each other. I used to meet
him outside the house, and tell my mother I was going out with
a girl friend. . . . When we got serious about each other, I told
my parents right away.

[CATHOLIC DAUGHTER]: I didn't tell my mother that I was dating
Raymond until I was serious about him, so she had no feelings
about it. . . . She knew about it right away when we became
serious, and I wrote and told my father at that time.

Not all of the parents who were unaware of the affair
initially became fully informed even at a later date:

[JEWISH DAUGHTER]: My parents didn't know from the beginning that we were seeing each other, or how often. Someone told my mother once that she'd seen us at the movies, and once my mother saw us at a party the crowd was having. . . . My mother had some inkling about us, but she never really wanted to believe it. They didn't know we were serious about each other until after we had run away to get married.

Other non-aware parents were cognizant of the relationship's beginning, but their subsequent image of the affair failed to keep abreast of its progress:

[JEWISH DAUGHTER]: When I first started dating my fiancé, I told my mother. . . . When we became serious about each other, I didn't tell my parents right away because of how they felt. My mother suspected he might be serious about me anyway. She was afraid he was getting serious, because she couldn't understand why he would see me so often when he wasn't getting any sex from it. . . . But she still didn't think that I'd get seriously involved with him, so I didn't tell her for quite a while.

[JEWISH DAUGHTER]: My parents knew from the beginning that we were seeing each other and how often, except for two occasions. In the middle of my senior year at high school they forbid me to see him, and it wasn't until a year later that they relented. I saw him during this time anyway. Then, afterward, we played down how often we were seeing each other even though they knew we were going out together. . . . After we decided to get married, we didn't tell them right away. We waited eight months.

To oversimplify our findings, there was a tendency for these parents to view the couple as acquaintances when they were actually friends, and as friends when they were actually lovers.

The fact that parental perception and reality failed to coincide had a number of consequences. Because they underestimated the seriousness of the affair, parents were less alarmed than they would have been otherwise. Had they realized fully what was happening, in all likelihood they would have brought more pressure to bear: ("If my parents had known how serious it was, there would have been a lot more objection." "They were not excited because they did not think anything was imminent.")

In turn, the disparity between actual and "appropriate" pressure affected the progress of the romance. When parents had no knowledge of the relationship in its beginning phase, the two partners were able to socialize at a time when their romance was very fragile and might have been terminated easily by outside forces. When these parents finally did learn what was happening, the partners—because they were now more engrossed in each other—were better equipped to withstand outside coercion. Consider now those parents who were aware of the relationship initially, but who failed to keep abreast of its development. In such instances, while the partners were exposed to pressure, presumably, they were exposed to less pressure than would have been the case otherwise.

In short, these romances were fostered in the sense that possible deterring forces were not fully mobilized. No doubt, there are many other occasions when non-approved behavior is promoted in the same manner, i.e., by a perceptual lag on the part of those who are in a position to exercise control. For example, parents may consider their sons merely "pranksters," when in reality they are juvenile delinquents; employers may believe their workers are merely piqued, when they are actually on the verge of resigning; political dictators may believe certain subgroups are only flirting with democratic ideas, whereas they are deeply committed. In each of these instances, the incorrect assessment of the situation by controlling forces will promote the further development of these "undesirable" tendencies.

Since the perceptual lag of parents was apparently of importance in fostering the marriages studied, it becomes pertinent to consider the reasons for the disparity between parents' image of the romance and the actual course of events. To begin with, a number of general factors undoubtedly contributed to this disparity. As their children mature, it is customary for parents to relax their vigilance and for the children themselves to demand more freedom. By the time their offspring reach marriageable age, parents know a good deal less about their activities; moreover, they are less likely to be informed of such activities—romantic or otherwise—at the time they actually accur.*

Apart from the fact that it is not customary for parents to stand guard over their children's romantic pursuits (at least when they are of marriageable age), there were additional reasons for the non-awareness of the parents in our group. Understandably, some of our subjects intentionally concealed their relationship out of fear that it would be threatened or dissolved if their parents learned of its existence:

[PROTESTANT DAUGHTER]: Neither family knew that we were of different religions when we got married. . . . As I look back now, we must have been scared to death of what our families were going to say. I guess we must have felt that if we didn't get married right away, they might object and make a lot of trouble.

However, fear for the future of the relationship was not the only consideration which prompted our subjects to

---

* Robert Merton's remarks concerning role-sets are pertinent in this connection: "The occupant of a status [in this case, the child] does not engage in continuous interaction with all those in his role-set. This is not an incidental fact, but is integral to the operation of role-sets. The interaction with each member (individual or groups) of the role-set is variously limited and intermittent; it is not equally sustained throughout the range of relationships entailed by the social status. This fundamental fact of role-structure allows for role-behavior which is at odds with the expectations of some in the role-set to proceed without undue stress. . . . To the extent that the role-structure insulates the status-occupant from direct observation by some of his role-set, he is not uniformly subject to competing pressures."[1]

conceal the romance from their parents. Occasionally, these individuals were motivated by other reasons; these are of considerable interest because, in leading parents to be unaware, they resulted in a situation conducive to the further development of the romance.

It will be recalled that some of our interviewees did not expect their relationship to become serious. This outlook—which, as noted, induced them to go on seeing the other—was also the reason their parents were not kept fully informed in some cases. A Catholic wife reasoned that it was pointless to mention the affair, since it would never "amount to much":

My mother didn't know from the beginning that I was seeing Carl, or how often we were seeing each other. This was because I felt, in the beginning, that he was just someone in the office and not worth mentioning.

However, once the relationship had become intimate, there were other considerations. One of our subjects, who debated at length whether or not to get married, was anxious to spare his parents what might turn out to be unnecessary anguish:

[JEWISH SON]: I knew a marriage would mean a storm, and it would raise a lot of unhappiness. . . . I felt I would rather not have my parents know anything until I was set in my own mind. I felt it would be better not to say anything to them.

On the other hand, there were some who were anxious to let their parents know what was happening, in the hope that they might accept the relationship, at least eventually. What is interesting about these cases is that, typically, the parents were neither immediately nor fully informed. Several of these young people, for example, felt they had a better chance of winning their parents over if the seriousness of the affair were divulged only slowly:

[PROTESTANT SON]: We were interested in getting our parents to accept this thing. . . . It was not our plan to suddenly break it to them. It was part of our strategy to let them see the handwriting on the wall before we started reading the words to them. We felt this was the best thing to do.

[JEWISH DAUGHTER]: I purposely didn't talk much about Ted or make an issue of him around the house, because I thought it was better to work on them slowly and get them used to the idea without too many head-on crashes.

Others, rather than divulge the seriousness of the affair by degrees, planned to bring their parents completely up-to-date, without further delay. But, significantly, their decision to act was postponed frequently. They kept waiting for an opportune moment to arrive:

[PROTESTANT DAUGHTER]: [*When you told your mother you were going to get married, how did she feel?*] Formerly, we had planned it for a weekend. But the weekend wasn't going well. That was because things like this were happening: I told her I wanted to take George to church with me. . . . She said, "You don't take a boy to church unless you're engaged to him." I said, "I guess that means we're engaged." Then she broke into tears. I said to George, "*Let's not tell her just now.*"

One further condition contributed to the lack of awareness of these parents. On several occasions, when the affair was concealed from one set of parents, this led the other set to be kept in the dark too:

[CATHOLIC DAUGHTER]: My husband hadn't squared it with his folks yet, and we didn't want to tell my family until we could tell everyone. . . .

[JEWISH SON]: [*Why didn't your wife tell her parents that she was going to get married?*] Since my folks didn't know, I felt it was only decent to keep everybody in the dark. I didn't want to make it look like a plot against my parents.

In summary, fear for the future of the relationship was not the only reason which led our subjects to conceal their affair. Their behavior was motivated by other (or additional) considerations as well, such as the desire to spare their parents unnecessary anguish or the hope that they might gain their parents' acceptance by breaking the news "gently." These considerations are significant because they led parents to be unaware of the "facts" and hence caused the couple to be confronted with less coercion. Knowingly or not, the subjects created a situation which promoted their marriage.

Factors Which Reduced the Impact of Parental Opposition

As we have seen, the opposed parents in our group were not fully aware of their child's cross-ethnic relationship as it progressed through its various phases. Their "ignorance," in turn, fostered the relationship because it led to a situation in which the young people were exposed to less coercion. However, this is not to say these couples were confronted with no resistance at all. We know this was far from the case: Their parents argued vociferously against the marriage; they took active steps to prevent the partners from becoming involved; and once they were involved, they did everything in their power to separate them.

At this point, we shall assume the existence of these parental pressures and focus on possible factors which may have minimized their effectiveness. More concretely, we shall view the situation from the standpoint of our subjects and raise the following question: Did these individuals behave in any particular ways or have any particular thoughts or feelings which reduced the impact of parental disapproval?

While we discussed many aspects of the parent-child relationship with these couples, this question was not clearly formulated until the interviewing was well under way. Only belatedly did we conclude that this might be a fruitful question to raise—fruitful, because it enables us to look upon the decision-making activity of our respondents as one instance of a more widespread phenomenon. The fact is that there are many occasions when an individual's behavior is not governed by the group to which he belongs, even though he is affirmatively oriented toward the group itself and toward those who occupy positions of control in that group. An employee may be warmly disposed toward his boss, a parishioner may have high regard for his pastor, and members of an adolescent gang may revere their leader —yet, it does not follow invariably that they will behave in accordance with the wishes of the latter (i.e., the boss, the pastor, etc.). In acting counter to the wishes of their parents, the individuals in our group behaved in a comparable fashion. With regard to all of these "nonconformists," we might wonder what, if any, special conditions were present which enabled them to act as they did.*

In the following passages we shall examine four of the ways in which the feelings, thoughts, and behavior of our interviewees appear to have minimized the impact of their parents' opposition.

To begin with, some of our respondents avoided exposing themselves to their parents' arguments—and in a number of different ways. When familial relationships became very strained at home, some of our subjects simply moved away and out of earshot of parental objections. Physical distance expedited the affair in a number of instances:

[JEWISH DAUGHTER]: But all of this—my going around with Paul—couldn't have happened if I had been living at home,

* This question (in somewhat different form) has been raised and discussed in the context of juvenile delinquency.[2]

because I couldn't have gone out with him so often without my parents . . . being very disapproving.

On those occasions when our subjects did not move away from home, at times they maneuvered matters so that they were not confronted with a constant barrage of objections. For example, a Protestant daughter, whose parents had qualms about intervening, took pains to see to it that they were not provided with an "opening": "I pretended not to see they were so upset, so that it wouldn't come to a head and so that we wouldn't argue." A Jewish boy, whose parents were less diffident, said:

I would not let my parents influence me. I would not let the subject come up. . . . Frequently, I would cut them off, or I would just walk out.

In another case, a Catholic boy managed to avoid his parents completely: "For a whole year I would come home, have supper, and then leave the house immediately."

Finally, whether the "child" is residing at home or away, parental objections may be cut short if the courtship is of brief duration. A Protestant wife, who was friendly with a couple contemplating intermarriage, recalled the advice she and her husband gave them: "When they . . . discussed it with is, we told them to do it quickly and they'd avoid a lot of discussion."

For the most part, parents who were opposed to their child's intermarriage were affirmatively oriented toward their background, and their objections to the marriage, at least to a significant degree, were an expression of their underlying commitment to their ethnic affiliation. They cherished the values of their group and wanted to see them perpetuated through the marriage of their child. However, our subjects (notably the Amenables) did not always share the values of their parents. They did not invariably feel that by outmarrying they were betraying their group or jeopardizing their cultural integrity or disgracing themselves socially. In the eyes of some, a chasm existed between their parents' generation and their own: ("My parents' thinking was antiquated." "There was such a different world between us." "My father's objections were foolish.") In short, these subjects were not moved by the moralistic objections of their parents. Since they had never assimilated ethnic group values, they felt no guilt in transgressing them.

In passing, it is interesting to note that several respondents believed their parents were wholly unaware of the divergence in outlook between them: "The greatest shock of all was that my parents had to come to grips with reality," a Catholic son stated. "I wasn't still a Catholic. They had never really believed this." And a Protestant daughter said: "The problem with my mother was to show her that I was quite different from what she hoped her daughter would be." In another case, a Protestant daughter pointed out that she was responsible for the fact that her parents failed to understand her as she grew older:

Way back when I was young, our disagreements were about my not wanting to do things they wanted me to do. I remember a big disagreement when I was about twelve, and they wanted me to come out of my shell and smile. There was a big campaign on. Then, when I was in high school . . . I was a pacifist and we disagreed violently about that. During college, I was a reformer. . . . Most of our disagreements were just a conflict of desires and not very deep. *When I started to disagree on fundamentals, I never told them how I felt.* Before that I gave in to them.

Aside from their underlying commitment to their respective ethnic group, it will be recalled that these parents took issue with the marriage because they felt it would give rise to a series of problems. While it is true that certain of these problems would not have been anticipated if these parents had been less attached to their heritage, others were more in the nature of possible "practical" difficulties which might arise. In other words, even though these parents had been indifferent to ethnic values, they still might have worried, for example, about whether the religious difference would lead to marital strife or whether their child would be rejected by his in-laws.

By and large, our subjects were not insensitive to these more pragmatic considerations. At the same time, a number of them viewed these fears on the part of their parents as exaggerated: "Whatever problems might occur, we thought we could solve them—otherwise we would never have gotten married." "We both knew the difference in our religions was going to be an obstacle, but we felt it could be surmounted." "I always felt confident that we could work out our difficulties, and that Larry and I understood each other."

On occasion, the respondent's personal experiences were responsible for his believing parental fears to be exaggerated. He had grounds for suspecting that certain problems they anticipated would not materialize. A Jewish daughter, whose parents prophesied that her friends would desert her if she intermarried, recalled:

I was never sure my parents weren't right or wouldn't be right some day, so it was nice to feel they were wrong, and it wasn't going to make any difference to my friends that I was marrying a Gentile. . . . The approval of my friends was important to me because it proved my parents were wrong—it was my ammunition against their attack that no one would associate with me if I married a Gentile.

Similarly, a Catholic daughter had reason to believe that anti-Semitism would not turn out to be a problem, as her parents predicted:

My mother used to argue with me a lot—mostly about the children, our standing in the community, and all the other social prestige reasons that are important to someone like her. . . . One of her arguments about social acceptance just didn't hold water with me *because my relationships before had never been affected by the fact that I knew Jews.*

With regard to the cases considered in the foregoing, there were two reasons why parental disapproval was less effective than it might have been. Because they were not committed to ethnic group values, some of these subjects were unmoved by their parents' moralistic objections. Others, because they believed that the problems their parents anticipated would not materialize, were overdrawn, or could be surmounted, considered their parents alarmists. However, parental objections lost their forcefulness for other reasons as well:

[JEWISH DAUGHTER]: It always seemed to me that almost everybody's parents objected to the person they were marrying, no matter if he had the same religion or not. Almost everybody's parents needles them in some way, like "why don't you go out with so-and-so?" I didn't feel this was really any too different from what my friends were going through with their parents.

Because this girl viewed parental dissatisfaction as a typical reaction, rather than a unique event, the substance of her parents' protests was, in all probability, taken less seriously.

Regardless of how our subjects reacted to the *content* of their parents' objections, some of them felt that their parents had no "right" to voice these objections (or, in fact, to voice any objections) to their romantic activities. These reactions are a reflection of certain cultural norms which are prevalent in our society. More specifically, the choice of a mate, in a normative sense, is up to the individual, and others are not permitted to intercede:

[JEWISH SON]: I felt who I was going out with was none of my mother's business. I was twenty-six years old at the time.

[CATHOLIC SON]: I said to my parents that here it is not like it is in the old country. In the old country they still bring you the girl to marry. I tried to explain things to them. I said that I knew that I would be happy, and that they should not stand in my way.

These subjects, and others like them, felt that the decision should reside in their hands alone, and that any intervention—whether it was expressed by verbal protest or otherwise—was morally "wrong." These sentiments neutralized the impact of their parents' disapproval:

[CATHOLIC DAUGHTER]: If two people want to get married—yes, no, or otherwise—it doesn't make any difference what people say. My father said lots of things, *but I never paid any attention.*

[JEWISH SON]: After that evening when my family said all those things [that his wife was ugly, ill-bred, slovenly, etc.] I saw my wife home. When I returned, both my parents were waiting up for me. They made it clear that if I persisted, they would disown me. . . . I called up my wife in order to see her, and I told her that I wanted to break it off. However, by the end of the weekend, I thought to myself that *it was time that I grew up. I can't do what my parents want me to all my life.*

Aside from prohibiting outsiders from intervening in matters of marital choice, American social mores decree that love should be the primary consideration in the choice of a mate:

[CATHOLIC DAUGHTER]: If you fall in love, you fall in love, and anything like religion makes no difference. I guess that's the way I felt about it.

[CATHOLIC DAUGHTER]: I felt that if you met someone you loved, you married him, no matter what his religion was.

The significance these subjects assigned to love probably led other issues dwelt upon by their parents to be assigned less importance by default. If love is so all-important, then the religion of their future children or how the two families get on matters a good deal less. However, these subjects were not merely saying that love was important, but that it was *rightfully* considered important. Since their parents were constantly interjecting other issues, the young people probably felt the relationship was being appraised in terms of standards which were singularly out of place and which ought not to be applied.

Finally, we were not surprised to find that democratic ideals and values had been thoroughly assimilated by some of our subjects. As a result, parental objections were viewed in a morally unfavorable light:

[JEWISH SON]: My parents said, "There are so many nice Jewish girls around—think what the neighbors will say about this." My attitude was one of heat. I was angry to think anyone would eliminate anyone else because of his religion.

In summary, we would assume that these inter-related sets of cultural norms—i.e., that neither parents nor anyone else should intervene in such matters, that love is the proper basis for choosing a mate, and that an individual should be judged on the basis of merit rather than ethnic affiliation—were of considerable importance in accounting for these marriages. These norms led certain of our subjects to feel that their behavior was morally above reproach, while that of their parents very definitely was not; in so doing, they shielded the young people from the full impact of their parents' coercion.

Moreover, not only may these norms weaken the effectiveness of parental opposition, but they may occasionally lead parental disapproval to become a facilitant, rather than a deterrent, to the marriage. The individual's anger at the conduct of his parents may be mingled with a sense of righteous indignation, which incites him to act in ways which are contrary to their wishes. In our group there were two cases (and perhaps others that we were not aware of) in which this probably occurred. A Catholic daughter remarked: "I think their opposition made me feel dogmatic toward them, and I was more positive about what I wanted to do." And a Protestant son said: "Maybe I was somewhat calloused about my mother's objections. There was a certain amount of resentment against her feeling this way about my wife."*

Aside from the cultural norms noted, the behavior of parents was morally condemned on other grounds as well. In reading through the interviews, we were impressed with the frequency with which our subjects discounted the manifest content of their parents' objections. In these instances (and there were over a dozen), the Jewish-Gentile issue was considered merely the ostensible reason for their elders' opposition. As they saw it, an entirely different set of considerations was really responsible for their behavior. It is worth adding that our respondents' remarks in this connection were wholly gratuitous: We did not ask them to probe beneath their parents' exterior, to unearth any underlying reasons for their opposition.

A number of these individuals stated emphatically that their parents would have objected to anyone they chose: ("My father wouldn't have liked anyone I married." "There would have been a certain amount of objection no matter who I married.") Others commented as follows:

* Perhaps the full significance of the norms we have noted can best be appreciated if we think of the plight of individuals in a familistic society (e.g., India or China) who are in a similar predicament. Certainly, it is less likely that the wishes of parents would be flouted in such situations.

[JEWISH SON]: My father's opposition was a terribly neurotic action or attitude on his part.

[JEWISH DAUGHTER]: My mother was violently against it. Before I even went out with him, I told her I had my eye on a Gentile boy, and she said, "Oh, no!" My mother referred to it as one of the tragedies of her life. *She likes to be a martyr.*

[PROTESTANT DAUGHTER]: The real reason I feel my father objected was that he wanted me as a daughter. He wanted to keep me in line. It would make him feel younger if I wasn't married. *It was pure selfishness.*

We shall by-pass the question as to whether there were valid grounds for these allegations. There may have been ample evidence for these "diagnoses"; on the other hand, these allegations may have been rationalizations for the most part, i.e., beliefs constructed by our subjects to justify their behavior.

However, whatever their basis, once these beliefs were held (and assuming they were arrived at before and not after the marriage), they discredited the behavior of those who were trying to put an end to the affair. In the eyes of these subjects, the conduct of their parents stemmed from illegitimate motives and intentions; or, put another way, from motives and intentions which are socially proscribed in this particular situation. For example, it is clear that parents who wish their child to remain single forever and who raise objections to any prospective mate are condemned in the eyes of the world. Again, parental protests are not apt to elicit much sympathy when those who are objecting are viewed as "selfish," "neurotic," or "playing the role of a martyr."

In conclusion, these various imputations presumably expedited the marriage, because, like the cultural norms considered previously, they put parental behavior in a morally objectionable light. *

Our respondents were not questioned as to how they had believed their parents would react as the romance continued, that is, whether they thought their parents' hostility would continue or diminish in intensity. Nevertheless, this question merits consideration, because if our subjects had expected parental opposition to subside, there was less cause for them to be so concerned over their parents' immediate reactions. And if they were less concerned, then the coercion to which they were exposed had less of a deterring effect. Lack of data prevents us from investigating this process in any detail. However, unsolicited remarks in this connection were scattered throughout our interviews and are worth noting briefly.

But before we turn to this matter, let us see whether parental feelings actually did undergo any change during the premarital stage. Over half of the subjects whose parents were opposed to their intermarriage were asked to compare the opposition felt by their parents at two different stages— when the parents first learned the relationship was serious and at the time of the marriage. As can be seen from Table 7, there was a tendency for parental opposition to subside, and at the time of the marriage less than half of these parents were strongly or moderately opposed to it. In terms of individual histories, roughly six out of ten of these parents became less disapproving as the romance progressed. The remarks of other of our respondents who were

---

* The pattern of behavior described here provides an instance of what Sykes and Matza, in their article on juvenile delinquency, term the "condemnation of the condemners." They write: "The delinquent shifts the focus of attention from his own deviant acts to the motives and behavior of those who disapprove of his violations. His condemners, he may claim, are hypocrites, deviants in disguise, or impelled by personal spite. . . . The validity of this jaundiced viewpoint is not so important as its function in turning back or deflecting the negative sanctions attached to violations of the norms."[3]

**Table 7. Degree of Parental Opposition at Two
Stages of the Courtship**

Degree of Opposition	On Learning the Relationship Was Serious	At the Time of the Marriage
Strong	70%	27%
Moderate	20	17
Mild	10	41
None	—	15
	100%	100%
Number of sets of parents	(29)	(29)

not asked directly to make this comparison led us to believe that their parents had reacted similarly.

We are primarily concerned, however, with whether these (or other) changes in parental attitudes had been *anticipated* by our subjects (or their partners). This occurred in at least several instances:

[PROTESTANT DAUGHTER]: I think what made my going through with the marriage easier was that I never questioned my family's love for me. Through thick and thin they had stood by me, and I thought they would on this finally.

[JEWISH DAUGHTER]: I felt concerned about my parents' opposition because we were a close family. However, I didn't want to give Sidney up. But I felt that even if I did marry him, I wouldn't lose them.

[CATHOLIC DAUGHTER-IN-LAW]: [*How did you happen to stay together?*] I realized, I think, the seriousness of his parents' objections, but I felt that once we were married, his family would not disown him. Rational people don't do that sort of thing. I've heard of a few families that did it, but I didn't think his family was that irrational. I thought the whole problem would be eliminated soon after we were married.

We infer that some of our other subjects had similar expectations, since they tried to bring their parents "around."

Presumably, such efforts would not have been made, if these subjects had concluded that their parents would be adamant—that there was no possibility of their being swayed.*

A number of considerations led our subjects to believe their parents would become more accepting. Some believed that their parents' resistance would subside once the latter concluded that any further efforts to prevent the marriage would be futile. We cannot definitely assert that this belief was held by our respondents; yet, when asked why their parents did in fact become more accepting, they attributed their acquiescence to the futility of prolonging the struggle:

[JEWISH DAUGHTER]: My mother changed her feelings when she realized I was in love with him, and there was nothing she could do about it. Then she saw it was no use fighting any more.

[PROTESTANT DAUGHTER]: The turning point came when I told my mother I would marry him no matter what happened. She saw I meant it, and it was no use opposing it.

At the same time, a few respondents acknowledged that the "acceptance" of their parents was probably only skin-deep:

[CATHOLIC DAUGHTER]: My parents and I had been through the whole business, and they had become resigned to the fact that we were getting married. They expressed all their opposition, until they came to the point of realizing that it was going to be, and they might as well get used to it. It was a matter of resignation to the inevitable. Their actual feeling did not change a bit.

Even though parents felt they might succeed in separating the couple ultimately, they may have become increasingly wary of attempting to do so. Clearly, their efforts might alienate their child and his partner, should the marriage take place. Rather than face the possibility of an

* The precise nature of these efforts will be described below.

estrangement, they may have become less disapproving, at least overtly. Again, we cannot be certain that these considerations entered into the thinking of our subjects and led them to expect that their parents' opposition would end. Still, when asked why the older generation did in fact become resigned, fear of alienation was cited as one of the reasons:

[JEWISH SON]: My parents were afraid they might lose me. It is true they felt strongly against my marrying a Gentile, but not strong enough to risk losing me by making a tremendous issue of it.

[JEWISH SON-IN-LAW]: My wife's mother opposed it, but she was afraid to oppose it too much, because the thing might bounce back. It might boomerang.

[JEWISH DAUGHTER]: My mother's feelings changed. . . . It was too much of a sacrifice for her to lose confiding in me. She would rather lose her principles than me.

It is worth adding that the respondent quoted above was an only child and, as such, was in a very strategic position *vis à vis* her mother. Since it is a greater blow for parents to become estranged from an only child than from one who has siblings, the former is able to exert greater control over his parents. In this connection, note the remarks of another only child who did not fail to take advantage of her position:

[PROTESTANT DAUGHTER]: My mother had to come around or feel that she would lose me. I was the last thing she had. I always knew this all my life and played my cards accordingly.

It has been suggested that some of our interviewees expected parental resistance to decrease, either because their parents believed further efforts to terminate the affair would be futile, or because they were fearful of an ensuing estrangement. On occasion, there were more specific considerations that led our subjects to anticipate that their parents might become more accepting. Two of our respondents felt they had been given a preview of their parents' future reactions. A Jewish daughter took into account the fact that similarly situated parents who lived in her neighborhood had become reconciled in the end:

A friend in the neighborhood, an older girl, married a non-Jew. Her mother ran through the streets screaming and all that baloney. Then, two weeks after the wedding, they were home living with the in-laws and everything was just fine. Her father even took him into the business. *So I figured no matter how much opposition my parents felt, it would be like that after the wedding, and everything would be fine.*

Another respondent was reassured by the fact that her own parents, having been confronted by the same situation before, had finally accepted it:

[PROTESTANT DAUGHTER]: Oh, yes, I anticipated my parents would feel opposed—because they felt the same way when my brother married a Catholic girl. But my brother managed to get through this cold-shoulder treatment, so I figured I could, too. My father insisted then that he wouldn't go to the ceremony, but on the day of my brother's wedding he got all dressed up and went. *So I knew it all could be done, in spite of how they felt.*

Many of our subjects, including some who felt their parents might come around "on their own," actively sought to placate them. While they were not asked (at least, not in any systematic manner) precisely how they attempted to accomplish this, several supplied this information spontaneously.

One of the principal ways in which these subjects sought

to placate their parents was to assure them that their religion, and not their partner's, would prevail in the event of a marriage. To this end, they tried to extract some kind of religious commitment from their future mates, such as an agreement with regard to the religious training of their future children. The efforts of the Reluctant in this connection were depicted earlier in another context. To the degree that these efforts derived from his parents' opposition, they constituted an attempt to appease his parents.

A number of these subjects felt that if their parents got to like the partner, their hostility would lessen, and some arranged to bring them together for this purpose:

[CATHOLIC DAUGHTER]: We hoped that if my fiancé kept coming back, my parents might come around, so we waited two years to get married.

[JEWISH SON]: I tried to get my parents to see things my way. I went so far as to have them meet my wife. . . . In fact, I arranged to bring them together quite frequently.

In passing, it is interesting to compare the conditions which initiated these contacts with the conditions which brought the Reluctants into contact with their partners. About half of these couples, it will be recalled, found themselves in the same institutional setting and, as a result of this, a number of them later established a more intimate relationship. However, there were no analogous forces which might serve to bring the individual and his future in-laws together and lead them to become favorably disposed toward each other. If the two were to meet and become friendly, the services of a third party would be required. In a sense, the meetings engineered by these subjects were intended to perform a function similar to that of an institutional setting.

We were interested, in pursuing this matter further, in finding out what happened after the individual and his prospective in-laws had been brought together by the "third party." Had the "third party" stood idly by in the belief that his parents could not fail to be impressed by his partner, or had he taken special steps to "sell" his future mate? In at least several instances, we found that our subjects had indeed tried to manipulate the situation. For example, as noted previously, on a few occasions the partner's ethnic identity was hidden from parents initially, in the hope that the latter would be less adamantly opposed to the marriage if they grew to like the partner before they learned of his religious affiliation.

Again, efforts were made by our subjects to present their partners in the most favorable light. A Protestant son recalled: "I tried to influence my mother by making her association with my wife pleasant over a period of time, going out to dinner . . . and building up my wife in front of her." Another subject explained more fully how she tried to set her husband off to best advantage:

[PROTESTANT DAUGHTER]: One evening, my uncle, my mother, George, and myself all had a talk. We went over all the things that were important to us—why we had to have a Jewish home and a Jewish family. I felt that if George could show his strength there, they would accept him better. So, although it was easier for me to talk to my relatives, I referred all the questions to him, and he answered them all instead of me. I did not do any talking at all that evening.

Of course, the partner himself may have taken pains to make a good impression, as evidenced in the following comments made by a Jewish wife with regard to her husband:

He used to bring gifts to my mother, maybe to blind her and make her forget he wasn't Jewish. At Christmas he brought gifts to everyone in the family. He was always very nice to my mother.

There was one other way in which these subjects sought to make their parents become more accepting. They tried to effect a fundamental change in their outlook—more specifically, to make them more tolerant of the outgroup:

[JEWISH DAUGHTER]: I spent a lot of time telling them about happy intermarriages; about such groups as the Ethical Culture Society and the Community Church; and about the favorable attitudes of people they respected. . . . I tried to show them that things in the U.S. were different from what they had known in Germany.

[PROTESTANT DAUGHTER]: I tried to get my parents to see things my way as best I could. I never really sat down and discussed it with either of them. It was hopeless to try to talk about something like this with my parents. However, I tried to influence them . . . by introducing them to Jewish food and they liked it. I cooked some of the dishes for them I had learned from my husband's mother.*

To summarize, some of our subjects felt their parents would eventually become more accepting (if not during the premarital stage of the romance, then after the marriage had taken place). While only a few said as much, we can infer that others, namely, those who made efforts to win their parents over, felt the same way. In all probability, such efforts would not have been made if these subjects had believed there was no hope of swaying their parents. Finally, and most important, if these subjects expected

---

* Clearly, after the marriage, repeated contact between the in-laws and the partner may lead the latter to be viewed in a more favorable light. A Jewish daughter, whose mother was "violently against the marriage" right up to the wedding, remarked: "I think my parents and Charlie like each other now. I think my mother feels differently now that we are married. Before we were married, she never spoke to him for a long time. Once we were married they became friendly. She even tells her friends that Charlie has a fine character. They seem to enjoy each other's sense of humor, and when he says something funny and other people haven't heard it, she stops and makes him repeat it. . . . [*How did this change of attitude come about?*] I think it's because she never bothered to get to know him until after we were married."

parental opposition to subside, there was less cause for them to be excessively concerned over their parents' immediate reactions. And if they were less concerned, the coercion to which they were exposed had less of a deterring effect.

Our discussion of parental opposition was predicated on the question of how these romances were able to develop within settings which were so hostile to their existence. More specifically, we wanted to know whether particular factors obtained which made parental opposition less effective than it might have been. To review our findings very briefly, the parents' image of the affair failed to keep abreast of its actual course. To this degree, the couple was exposed to less pressure than would have been the case otherwise. In addition, a number of conditions reduced the effectiveness of whatever pressure parents did bring to bear: Our respondents tried not to expose themselves to the objections of their parents; they viewed certain objections as unimportant or exaggerated; they regarded others as illegitimate; and, finally, they felt their parents would "come around" in the end. Any one—or a combination—of these factors increased the possibility that the courtships of our subjects would eventuate in marriage.

THE RELUCTANT AND
HIS FRIENDS

10 . . . *The Role of Friends*

AT THE pre-interview stage, we assumed that the outcome
of the Reluctant's courtship would be affected by his relationship with his parents. The same assumption was held
with respect to friends. That is, we felt that whether the
Reluctant would become interested in his partner, then involved, and finally married would depend, in some measure, on the way his friends felt about the affair and the
way in which they interacted with our subject. How these
courtships were, in fact, affected by Reluctant-friend relationships will occupy our attention in this chapter.*

During the interviewing, our general aim was to obtain
a summary picture of how the Reluctant's friends felt about
the attachment and their relationship with the Reluctant
during the courtship period. At the same time, we had several suppositions which led us to focus our inquiry around
certain topics. We felt it likely that the Reluctants would
be surrounded by approving friends, who, in turn, would
have an important bolstering effect. Certainly, this is not
an unreasonable expectation, in view of the conflict situation the Reluctants were in: They were drawn to their partners but simultaneously motivated to withdraw. Since the

* Our discussion will focus only upon the twenty-nine Reluctants in
our group, unlike the previous section on parents, which included some
Amenables.

Reluctants did go through with the marriage, we thought it probable that they had received support which had enabled them to resolve this conflict, and that this support had come from some area of their primary environment.

With these considerations in mind, first we asked each of our subjects whether he had any *close* friends during the period in which he was going out with his future mate. Since the opinions of casual friends are apt to carry less weight, we only attempted to solicit information about those specifically labeled as "close."* If he had one or more friends who fit this description, he was asked the following questions about each:

1. How did your friend feel about intermarriage in general?

2. How did he feel, in particular, about your attachment?

3. Did you have any conversations bearing upon these topics? If so, what was the nature of their content?

4. Finally, when his circle of friends was approving (which was the case in all but three instances), he was asked to evaluate the significance of its support.

In gathering information about friends, we had to rely, of course, upon the reports provided by our subjects. Therefore, we cannot be sure that the feelings and viewpoints of friends were accurately depicted. In particular, our subjects may have failed to recognize attitudes of disapproval, since it is likely that friends who disapprove will try to convey the impression they are less disapproving than is actually the case.[1] No doubt, their "act" will deceive the other some of the time. Nevertheless, for the purposes of our study, we shall view the Reluctant's image of his friends' feelings as coinciding with the way these friends actually felt.

To provide an overview of these friendship circles, of the 29 Reluctants in our group, there were 5 who had no close

---

* This question should be distinguished from one presented and discussed earlier, in which the respondents were asked about the ethnicity of their close and/or casual friends when they (the respondents) were past high school age.

friends; 21, whose circle was approving (or predominantly approving); and 3, whose circle was disapproving. In the following passages we shall examine the Reluctant's relationship with his friendship circle and with certain of its members. Particular heed will be paid to the effect of these relationships on the affair—more specifically, the extent to which the affair was promoted or deterred by these friendships.

The Support of Approving Circles

Nearly all of the Reluctants who were the nuclei of approving circles felt that the support of their friends had been of considerable importance. This is brought out by the following excerpts, which are more or less typical of the responses made by this group. We have also included some of the Reluctants' preliminary comments, in which they described their friends and the discussions they had with them, in order to convey more graphically the meaningfulness of their friends' support:

[CATHOLIC WIFE]: I discussed the problem we had with our families with my two friends [*one Catholic, one Protestant*]. Like the nice friends they were, they said, "Go ahead and do what you feel is best." I feel friends certainly are important in a situation like this. It's very nice to feel they support you and are behind you. And it did help me in reaching a decision. . . . If your friends and you are the same religion, and your friends talk against the group your husband belongs to, you feel ashamed of your friends. But it makes it hard for you to feel the same about your husband as you did before.

[JEWISH WIFE]: My closest friend [*Jewish*] was on our side all the time and felt, like me, that she'd intermarry if she were in my situation. She had nothing against intermarriage. We talked about my situation a lot because she had some of the same troubles. Her parents didn't like her boy friend, even though he was Jewish, and they had been very opposed to her getting married. We were always together, Doris and I, and we talked a lot about this whenever something new came up—we talked about how my parents would feel, what to do about children, and how we were going to get married. . . . I think it's very important for people in this situation to have their friends' approval. Well, actually, their approval isn't necessary, but their support. You need somebody on your side. . . . All of our friends were behind us in this matter. They protected us from my parents—they lied for us and shielded us. . . . However, [their approval] made no difference when it came to making a decision to get married. Maybe it did, but I don't think so.

[CATHOLIC WIFE]: I had two close girl friends during the time I was going with my husband. They were both my shoulders to cry on. . . . Kay [*Catholic*] felt she couldn't enter a mixed marriage herself, but she didn't exclude all others from doing this just because she wasn't capable of it. In our case, she felt we should get married. We talked all the time about this—about everything, our feelings, other people's feelings, and so on. . . . As for Carol [*Jewish*], I don't remember how she felt about intermarriage, or that she had any particular feelings. . . . [*How did she feel about you and your husband?*] Mostly, she just used to listen. I don't remember her expressing any opinion. She was one of those people who always brought up the other point of view, in order to make others think about their point of view— but this did not mean she was set against it. We used to discuss my problems frequently, but always from the philosophical point of view, ending up in a big discussion of religion. . . . Yes, I would say my friends were behind me in this—a great deal. [*How important is it for people in this sort of situation to have their friends' approval or support?*] About approval, I don't know if it's important. But support is very important. They can support you, even if they have reservations. It was very important to me to have my friends' support.

[CATHOLIC WIFE]: I had three close friends while I was going with Herbert. . . . I remember saying once to Joan [*Catholic*],

"I'm so worried about marrying a Jew." I loved her for the answer she gave me. She said, "If Bernard Baruch proposed to you, would you care he was Jewish!" That showed me so well how she felt and made me feel good. She thought Herbert was a fine person and that was all that was important. . . . Sue [*Catholic*] thought I was smarter than any of my friends because by marrying out of the group I got someone so attractive. . . . Betty [*Protestant*] was to be my maid of honor. She showed great concern about what I was doing. But we talked about it, and I convinced her that I really knew what I was doing and felt it was the right thing, and then she agreed wholeheartedly to be in the wedding. . . . I talked to all three of these girls quite often about my problems. We discussed my family's attitudes and his family's attitudes, my worries about marrying him, and what was going to happen to our children. . . . I feel it means a great, great deal to people in this sort of situation to have their friends' support. It was very important to me.

Her further remarks, in which she questioned how her friends really felt and revealed her dependence upon them, point up her feeling that their overt endorsement was of importance:

Although none of them expressed any opposition, I was still not sure exactly how they felt and what they were going to do. I was scared to death until the invitations started to come in after the marriage. I often felt that I had bitten off more than I could chew, and that maybe when it came to asking us to dinner parties, they would find it just as easy *not* to ask us.

[JEWISH HUSBAND]: My three closest friends [*all Jewish*] were in the Army at the time. We did not discuss this personally, but we discussed it at length in the mails. . . . As for Carl, he felt we were being unduly persecuted. He was all for us . . . and felt we should get married despite the opposition. I described the situation to them—the objections of our parents and our own feelings about the matter. They felt that our feelings and our future were more important than consideration for our parents. . . .

Yes, I felt their support was important. [*How would you have felt if your friends had been against it?*] I would not have wanted to alienate my friends as well as my parents. We were a close group and still are.

Occasionally, the subject mentioned his friends before he was asked about them explicitly. For example, when asked if anything in the situation had helped him and his wife to stay together, a Jewish boy replied:

Yes, a mutual friend [*Jewish*]. This fellow and myself had been buddies for fourteen years. He was very much in favor of it, and he and his wife were one of the couples we went with when we became serious. Mary and I had grown to know and like the two of them very much. During the weeks when we were on the outs, my wife went over to their house one night, and they had a four- or five-hour conversation. Two days later, my friend and myself happened to take a ride together, and he spoke strongly in favor of our love conquering this and the ridiculousness of just throwing it away. . . . He realized the toughness of the situation, but he was aware of the value and importance of love. His idea was that, by the nature of the love alliance, a solution [to our religious differences] would have to come, through the process of give and take.

The following case is of interest, because it shows how an individual may become surrounded by friends whose feelings toward intermarriage are at odds with his own. The Protestant husband in question grew up and went to college in Iowa; during this time he had very little contact with Jews. After that, he attended a school of social work in New York City and worked in a Jewish neighborhood house at the same time. Referring to this period of his life, he said: "By this time I had lost, intellectually at least, a lot of my strong feelings about the correctness of Christianity as the best religion. . . . Nevertheless, I still had a tremendous amount of residual, emotional feeling that I would be more comfortable marrying someone from a

Protestant background [for both religious and social rea-
sons]." From his description of his friends, it would appear
that he became encircled by a group whose views toward
intermarriage were more liberal than his own. Of his three
close friends, one was a "nonsectarian" Jew who interdated
and who previously had been infatuated with a Gentile
woman; one was a Jew whose wife was the product of an
intermarriage; and the last, a Protestant who was his roommate, was "the last person in the world to object to intermarriages" and was friendly with a number of interracial
couples. Describing their reactions to his courtship, he said,
"All three supported me. . . . Their sympathies were entirely
with me, rather than even hinting there was something to
the arguments of our parents." Referring to his wider circle,
inclusive of the friends just mentioned, he observed:

They were a crowd of social workers and folk dancers. . . . The
whole group was mixed religiously and racially. I suppose the
religious feeling in that group was rather agnostic; politically,
they were liberal. I expect this had a lot to do with my going
through with the marriage.*

It is interesting to take note of several instances in which
the approval of friends was assigned very little importance.
In one case, a Catholic wife had discussed with her two
friends (Catholics) such things as whether she and her
husband would have arguments about religion, and how
the two would get along, in general. When asked if her
friends' reassurance had been important, she replied:

* Since there is much evidence to the effect that, in general, friends are
apt to hold similar opinions and attitudes,[2] we might expect friends to hold
similar views with regard to intermarriage. It is interesting, therefore, that
many of the Reluctants in our group had friends whose outlook toward
intermarriage was, seemingly, more liberal than their own. The case just
cited suggests one of the ways in which this may come about. The Reluctant, finding himself in a new environment and hoping to develop new
friendships, may be unable to locate persons who share his general outlook. Rather than remaining completely isolated, he may prefer the com-
panionship of those whose views are uncongenial, at least in certain
respects.

I felt I knew what I was doing. If my friends had disagreed with me and I had to choose, I would naturally pick my husband over my friends. [*Do you think it helps to have your friends behind you?*] Yes, naturally, you feel better. But it wasn't important to me.

If we accept these cursory remarks at face value, perhaps the relative unimportance of her friends' opinions can be explained, in part, by other aspects of her courtship. For one thing, her partner, who had never been a religious Jew, agreed to raise the children as Catholics.* Second, the girl's parents accepted the relationship very early in the courtship, and perhaps their support made her less dependent on the opinions of others. The remarks of two Amenables are of interest in this connection:

[CATHOLIC WIFE]: If my parents had objected, I would have turned to my friends for support.

[PROTESTANT WIFE]: If your parents are opposed and you have to give them up when you marry, you need your friends very badly. You don't want to give up your whole past when you marry.

Turning to another case in which friends were reputed to play a minor role, a Catholic engaged woman, who had met her fiancé at law school, remarked:

My law school friends all liked him. . . . Our problem was common knowledge among many of our friends. We discussed it with them a lot—mostly problems of how our parents were behaving and what religion the children should be. . . . We decidedly got support from them. They all knew we had these problems with our parents and were behind us on that.

When asked to appraise the importance of her friends' support, she replied, "The opinion of my friends was not im-

* This agreement was, in fact, reached before the marriage, although we do not know at what stage.

portant at all. Of course, one wants one's friends to approve, but it wouldn't have made any difference if they'd been violently against it." If, again, we take these remarks at face value, how can the relative unimportance of her friends' feelings be explained? Had this girl's parents become more accepting, as they had in the case described earlier? And had her partner agreed (or indicated that he would agree) to a Catholic home? Quite the contrary. At the time of the interview, this subject's parents were still violently opposed to the marriage, and questions about the children were still unresolved: "We haven't reached a decision on their religious education. They won't be brought up as Jews, but we haven't made up our minds to bring them up as Catholics. We are both violently against Ethical Culture and other such 'religions.' The children will probably wind up with a lot of both religions." Furthermore, from what she said of her fiancé, who was not interviewed, it would appear she had little reason to hope that he would ever agree to raise them as Catholics. He was the son of Jews who kept a kosher home; he had gone to a Hebrew elementary school, which had "great influence" on him; and his religion "meant more" to him that it did to his parents.

In view of these circumstances—i.e., that her parents were bitterly opposed to the marriage and that she might have to sacrifice her religion—we would have predicted that her friends' endorsement of the affair would have been of vital significance. Perhaps its relative unimportance can be attributed to the fact that this woman was simply a more independent, autonomous type of person than others in our group.

However, other possibilities are worth considering as well. For one thing, because of certain characteristics of the courtship setting, the person who is being influenced by his friends may not recognize the full extent of their influence. On the one hand, the actor is expected to reach a marital decision independently, without outside aid or advice. On the other hand, since the decision is a vitally important one and the individual may be plagued with doubts, he may be especially anxious to "sound out" others whose opinion he respects. In such a situation, we would suggest that whatever influence is being exerted will be more dimly perceived than would be the case otherwise. Cultural norms which demand that the individual be self-reliant may prevent him from discerning the role played by others.

Second, regardless of the cultural norms which obtain, when the individual is surrounded by friends who uniformly approve of his actions, the very pervasiveness of their approval may lead him to underestimate their influence. Because the subject is not exposed to divergent, contrasting viewpoints, it may become more difficult for him to appreciate the role played by the many who are sympathetically disposed. The responses of several Amenables who were asked to appraise the importance of their friends' approval are of interest in this connection. At first, they dismissed its importance; then they backtracked and said that perhaps their friends' approval was not unimportant after all:

[PROTESTANT WIFE]: I don't know that my friends' approval really helped me in reaching a decision, but the decision was made in this whole atmosphere which was favorable. Yes, I guess it did help.

[CATHOLIC WIFE]: It was not really important to me how my friends felt. But in a way I guess it was. I just assumed they would feel the way I did [*i.e., approve*], so there was really no issue.

To summarize our comments up to this point, generally, there was a good deal of discussion between the Reluctant and his approving friends, and the respondent's dilemma was apt to be well aired. Moreover, with a few exceptions, the Reluctants felt that their friend's (or friends') encouragement was of some importance in pushing them closer to the altar.

It is appropriate to interject a few remarks about mutual friends at this time. While we made no effort to investigate the specific role they may have played in promoting the courtships of our subjects, friends of this sort may greatly facilitate a marriage. More concretely, we would expect that, typically, a courtship would be fostered more by a mutual friend who approves than by a non-mutual friend who approves, and for these reasons:

1. A mutual friend may play an important role right at the start—at a time when the partners' relationship is very tenuous. After their meeting (which, of course, their friend may have arranged), he may actively encourage the relationship. Yet, even if he makes not the slightest effort to advance the affair, his very existence will have an effect. Each of the partners will infer that there must be "quite a lot" to the other. Otherwise, how could their friend's warm feelings for the partner be explained?

2. The partners will not be tempted to question the sincerity of their friend's approval of the relationship, as they might if their friend were not *also* a friend of their partner's. For example, one of our subjects took it for granted that her companions were approving, since they were also long-standing friends of her husband's:

Yes, I would say my friends agreed with me in what I was doing. And mostly, they were Don's friends, too—so, *of course,* they agreed with me.

3. A mutual friend—or, more likely, a network of mutual friends—may promote the relationship, even unintentionally. For one thing, they may be responsible for the fact that the partners repeatedly find themselves in each other's company. Moreover, if the two are inclined to separate, the

fact that they are surrounded by mutual friends may deter them. To part when there is a good chance that they will meet frequently in the future may prove awkward and prompt some second thoughts about breaking off the affair.

The Influence of Mixed and Disapproving Circles

Let us now turn to those Reluctants whose social circle included one or more disapproving friends.* Here again, we shall be concerned with the interaction between the subject and his friends and, in this instance, the degree to which the latter constituted a retarding force. But first, a preliminary word about the types of Reluctants with whom we shall be dealing. There were four Reluctants in our group who had one disapproving friend and one Reluctant who had more than one, although the majority of their friends approved of the relationship. In addition, there were three Reluctants whose social circle was disapproving. We shall discuss these two categories of Reluctants separately, although, as we shall see, their relationships with their disapproving friends were similar.

Let us consider first the five instances where, although generally the Reluctant's social circle approved of his relationship, one or two friends were disapproving. In the first of these cases to be considered, the disapproving friend left the Reluctant's circle:

[JEWISH WIFE]: Sarah [*Jewish*] was definitely against intermarriages. She didn't think they would work out. The reason she felt this way was her feeling that the backgrounds of the people would be too different. Also, she felt strongly that it was a matter of principle, and that Jews should stick together. She

* Our interest in the individual's relationships with his disapproving friends derives in large measure from a paper by Lazarsfeld and Merton.[3]

was one of the few who knew about Vincent right from the beginning. But we never talked much about intermarriage, because she disappeared from our group and went to Israel to live.

Any pressure this friend might have brought to bear was thus precluded by her departure from the group. But of greater interest is the fact that her departure from the group was, seemingly, more than just a "fluke." Her going to Israel to live was quite in keeping with her ethnic convictions and illustrates an important, albeit obvious, point: When the values of two friends diverge, this very divergence, in leading the two to become separated, may prevent their influencing each other in the future.

In the next case, a Jewish male had two distinct friendship circles: "I have kept all of my old Jewish friends since I was eight. But after leaving high school I made new acquaintances of all religions—in college, in the Army, and in med school." He then described the reactions of his "newer" friends toward his courtship:

Jim [*a nonpracticing Catholic*] thought marrying Susan was a good idea. He was a rebel. He didn't think that mothers should tell sons what to do. He knew all about my situation. We talked about how my family felt, and the problems of intermarriage. ... Dan, who is a Quaker, was another enlightened person. He would say, "When are you going to break the bonds that hold you to your mother's apron strings?". . . . They both knew all about the situation. When I felt disheartened or blue, I would talk to them about it. [*When you stopped seeing Susan, did they influence you to go back to her?*] They did in a kind of joking way. They would say, "What are you hanging around here for? Why don't you call her up? What are you waiting for?"

He continued, "These two, of course, were my newer friends. I'm sure my older friends, the Jewish ones from my boyhood, probably felt differently. But they never said one

single thing to me about it." We cannot be sure, of course,
what would have happened if these disapproving friends
had verbalized their feelings (even though we assume, in
accordance with procedures outlined earlier, that our subject perceived the full extent of their disapproval). Had
they expressed their objections, the respondent might have
dropped them; or he might have ignored their objections
and retained them as friends. On the other hand, he might
have listened to them, been affected by what they had to
say, and terminated the relationship, partly as a result of
their influence. In other words, because they remained
silent, these disapproving friends exerted less of a retarding
influence than they might have. For this reason, we would
look upon their reticence—and they were reticent throughout the courtship—as constituting a condition which possibly promoted the affair. Viewed in another way, the composite influence to which this subject was exposed was not
simply a reflection of the *number* of approving and disapproving friends in his circle. Rather, his approving
friends, because they were much more verbal, were responsible for the aggregate influence becoming skewed toward the positive pole.

As mentioned earlier, the subject just discussed happened to have two distinct circles of friends, one of which
was approving and the other disapproving. However, the
phenomenon described may also occur when both approving and disapproving friends are members of the same
circle. Because they do not articulate their feelings, those
who disapprove may exert less influence than those who
approve of the relationship. Since none of the histories of
the Reluctants in our group were able to provide a good
illustration of this process, we have drawn on information
supplied by an Amenable:

[JEWISH HUSBAND]: In general, Bob [*Jewish*] did not like intermarriages. . . . His feelings against it are inbred; it is something

that is just not done. . . . I knew how he felt from when we were younger—most of the fellows didn't go with Gentile girls, they were afraid they would fall in love and marry. . . . No, I never talked with him about my particular situation, and he never said how he felt directly. Chuck [*Jewish*] thought intermarriages were all right. He was more liberal than Bob; he was inclined to be favorable. Yes, I talked with him about it—about parental difficulties and so forth. He felt the same way I did—he agreed with me.

In the following two cases, the Reluctants' disapproving friends verbalized their feelings, and the friendships deteriorated as a result. In one case, a Jewish male said of his close companion:

Jack [*Jewish*] did his best to talk me out of it. He said it was the worst thing I could do. He thought that I was really kidding about the whole affair. He took a strong interest in it and really tried to discourage me. . . . His objections were that it would not work out, that I had my parents to consider, and that my parents would be so upset they would disown me. . . . [*Did you talk with him often?*] Yes, to the point where I decided to avoid him for a while. At that particular point, he became a real nuisance.

The subject then explained why he had been so annoyed: "I felt I was the one to make up my mind about this thing." But, in addition, he felt that the difference between himself and his friend was not one which could be resolved:

I couldn't really answer his objections and argue back. It was not the type of thing that I could sit down and argue with him about. I felt that our conversations were pointless. . . . I became very irked about it.

In the second case, the friendship was not merely strained, but came to an abrupt halt:

[CATHOLIC WIFE]: Jane [*Jewish*] was very upset about us, and we don't see each other any more. She believes in preserving the nice Jewish boys for the nice Jewish girls. We had two violent arguments about intermarriage, and then that was the end of my friendship with her.

In both of these cases, the deterring influence of the disapproving friend diminished over time: The Reluctant became exposed to his objections less frequently, and, in any event, probably came to care less about his opinions. There is a similarity between these two cases and those in which the Reluctant's friends were reticent throughout the courtship. In both instances, the aggregate influences playing upon the Reluctant became skewed in a favorable direction, and to that degree the romance was promoted.

In the last case in this group, although the disapproving friend expressed her feelings, the friendship apparently suffered no ill effects:

[PROTESTANT WIFE]: Ellen [*Protestant*] didn't approve of my marrying Dan. She practically said it was on the rocks before we even got married. . . . She had had a friend who married a Jew, and it didn't work out and they got divorced—so she didn't think it was a good idea. But this didn't affect our friendship.

We might wonder why, in this instance, the friendship was not subjected to greater strain. Perhaps the fact that the friend's objections were practical (i.e., the marriage wouldn't work out), rather than normative, was significant. If the Reluctant felt that her friend's opposition was "legitimate," she may have been less offended by her negative reaction. In this connection, we would point out that when any of our subjects did become estranged from their disapproving friends, the latters' protests were apt to be of a nonpractical or normative character:

[PROTESTANT WIFE]: Jean [*Protestant*] disliked the Jews in general, because she had one unpleasant experience with a Jewish boy she had dated. She disliked him so much that she carried this over to Sam. This definitely caused a slight break in our relationship. We continued to be roommates and good friends, but it wasn't the same.

[PROTESTANT WIFE]: Cecile [*Catholic*] made some nasty remarks about his being Jewish, with the idea that you know how Jews are, but she never gave any reason or explained this. . . . I got very angry about how she felt about my husband, and I stopped seeing her.

Let us now turn to the three Reluctants who visualized their circles as predominantly disapproving. Although a consideration of these cases will not introduce any factors not touched upon previously, there is perhaps sufficient interest in relationships of this type to warrant their review. In the following passage, a Jewish wife describes her two close friends. One of them "spoke up" and was immediately dropped; the other was more discreet:

There was one fellow, a Jewish boy, I was very close to. We were like brother and sister. We bowled together. Once, after I was going out with my husband, I saw this boy at the bowling alley and I said, "Let's all go out together." He said, "No, he's not my kind." I've never spoken to him again. He was too close to me to say anything like that.

Nancy [*Jewish*] was my closest friend and came from a very religious home. She liked Herb, but thought that we would have a hard time. She felt intermarriage was wrong because there were so many problems involved. In general she disapproved, but she didn't try to influence me. . . . She didn't advise me, except to say that I should make sure the problems have all been solved beforehand because you can't solve them afterwards. [*How did she feel underneath?*] Underneath I'm sure she felt it would be better for me to marry a Jew.

Another Jewish wife described her two close friends as being very guarded in their comments:

Edith [*Catholic*] was my closest friend while I was going with my husband. She only went with Catholic boys and married a Catholic. [*How did she feel about intermarriage?*] I don't think she'd approve of it for herself, and I don't know how she felt about me. [*Did she ever say anything?*] No, the only thing I remember her saying was that she felt the children should be the same religion as the father.

Mabel [*Jewish*] only went out with Jewish boys, and she is marrying a Jew. She never saw any Gentile boy more than once. [*How did she feel about Paul and you?*] I don't think she was opposed to it. She never said I shouldn't marry him. We never talked about it. . . . Both of my friends never said anything either way about how they felt. I guess they felt it was none of their business.

If these Reluctant women felt that their circles were predominantly disapproving (and we have assumed this was the case), this factor can only have been a deterrent to the romance. However, because three of the four friends described hardly expressed their feelings, they hindered the relationship less than they might have. If, on the other hand, these friends had spoken up—and spoken up vociferously—it is possible that the marriage would not have taken place.

The last case to be considered is particularly interesting, because not only did the Reluctant's companions express their opposition fully, but, because these friendships did not deteriorate as a result, the friends were able to voice their disapproval over a considerable period of time.

[CATHOLIC HUSBAND]: I had four close friends. They were Italian Catholics and were very religious. At the time I was going with my wife, they were all single, although now three of them have married Italian Catholics who came from the same town they came from in Sicily. . . . They advised me not to marry my wife. They advised me against it and spoke to me about it all the time. They said the same things over and over again. They said I did not realize what I was doing.

His wife also had something to say about his friends:

Tony's friends were a pain in the neck. They were very opposed. . . . One day they all came to the house and told me Tony would lose his friends if I didn't quit, and that I should give up the idea of marrying him. The next day I told Tony it was all off because of what his friends thought about it.

Since our subject did not stop seeing his wife, we might have expected that he would have stopped seeing his friends. However, nothing even approximating this occurred. He explained why he was not more offended by the behavior of his companions:

They were really worried more about my parents than anything else. They were very close to my mother. They would see a lot of her because she was outside in front of the house a great deal. They talked with her a lot. . . . They understood my mother's viewpoint and they were thinking of her and what it meant to her. I realized that they were doing what they thought was best for me.

Because he felt his friends' resistance derived from legitimate concerns, that is, concerns for his and his mother's welfare, he was less resentful. And, once again, this is perhaps the reason these friendships were able to survive.

To summarize this section on the relationship between the Reluctant and his disapproving friends, the following patterns were noted: In one case, the disapproving friend left the Reluctant's circle; in several instances, he was reticent throughout the courtship; and in several others, he voiced his feelings. When the disapproving friend voiced his feelings, the friendship deteriorated on some occasions, while in others it suffered no ill effects (possibly because the friend's objections were felt to be legitimate). In discussing these patterns, we suggested that there was a tendency for disapproving friends to deter the romance less than they might have. To take another view of this matter, they retarded the romance less than approving friends promoted it.

In conclusion, the interest we have taken in disapproving friends should not obscure the fact that the large majority of our subjects were the nuclei of approving circles. Typically, the Reluctant's friends were sympathetic, and they did not hesitate to display their feelings. Their support, in turn, was of some consequence in bringing about the marriage.*

* In previously considering the child-disapproving parent relationship, we dwelt upon certain conditions which minimized the effectiveness of parental opposition. Some of these same conditions reduced the effectiveness of friends' opposition (e.g., the subject stopped exposing himself to his friend's protests; he questioned the legitimacy of his arguments). While further parallels (aside from a few exceptions) were not revealed by our data, they may, nonetheless, have been present. However, we would suggest that, typically, there will be certain differences in the way (or ways) an actor deals with a disapproving friend and a disapproving parent when the actor is equally close to both. We would expect him to break off the relationship with a friend; with parents, we would expect him to try to do any or all of the following: to conceal the romance from them; to immunize himself from their opposition; to win them over. Why should friends and parents be dealt with differently? For one thing, friends are replaceable. The actor can acquire new ones who are more sympathetically disposed. Secondly, external forces counteract any desire he may have to break away from his parents. Members of the family circle will move in rapidly to prevent a schism; and if one has already developed, they will probably do their utmost to heal it. Friendships, on the other hand, are not exposed to cohering forces of this nature and for this reason (among others) will more frequently come to an end.

SUMMARY

---

11 . . .   *A Review of*

Our Findings

IN THE COURSE of our investigation, various aspects of the courtships under surveillance were discussed separately, in order to facilitate their over-all study. Thus, the Reluctant's relationships with his partner, his parents, and his friends were conceptually sealed off from each other; then, within each of these divisions, certain topics were singled out for discussion. While some such procedure was necessary for purposes of our analysis, it must inevitably convey a very disjointed picture of the courtships of our subjects. Any sense of the continuity of the process is apt to be lost.

In an effort to make these courtships "come to life"—and as a means of reviewing our findings as well—we have constructed a case history which reflects the influences which promoted these marriages. (Influences which we hypothesized were operating have also been included.) We have tried to weave all of these elements into a single case—and, hopefully, in not too contrived a fashion. But first a word about the kinds of influences which were dealt with in the text. Some of these had an immediate and direct effect upon the courtship; others were indirectly related to it. In other words, we considered both *immediate antecedent conditions* and the *factors which were responsible for these conditions*. Nearly all the influences in the first category have been included in the "case history" which follows. Many of those in the second category have been omitted, however, because they are less germane to the immediate issues involved.

To repeat, the following case incorporates practically all of the primary influences we have described throughout this book. As such, it is hoped that it will "point up" the various processes depicted, and will impart some sense of the way these processes "added up" to bring about a marriage.

Our subject is a Jewish male.

If someone had told me five years ago I would marry a Christian, I'm sure I would have laughed in his face. The whole idea would have struck me as preposterous. Let me explain—it's not that I ever sat down and reached a decision that I would like to marry a Jewess—I just took it for granted I would. You see, I had grown up in a Jewish home, I'd always lived in Jewish neighborhoods, and all of my friends right through high school had been Jewish. As I say, I naturally assumed my wife would be Jewish, in the same way you assume your wife will be about your age or a little younger—certainly not someone ten years older than yourself. . . . Well, when you come right down to it, I suppose there were a lot of reasons for my wanting to marry a Jewish girl. Basically, I suppose I just liked the idea of being Jewish. There were a whole lot of things about it that were all mixed up in my mind—the excitement of the holidays when we were kids; the family feeling when all the aunts, uncles, and cousins would get together; the history of the Jews and how they had survived so much; and lots of other things, too. Well, when it came to marrying, I naturally wanted to have a Jewish home. I don't mean the girl had to be orthodox and keep a strict kosher home. I had grown away from a lot of the old customs—they had always seemed kind of silly and oppressive. I don't know how to say it—but I wanted to marry someone I could feel close to, someone who would understand and share my way of life; someone who would raise my children to be decent, self-respecting Jews. As for a Christian girl filling this bill—well, it was even crazy to think about! . . . Then there was the question of my parents. The idea of a Jew marrying a Gentile—and this was true of all the Jewish parents in our neighborhood—was unthinkable. It was the worst kind of thing you could do. I knew my parents would be broken hearted if I married out—particularly, since I was an only child. I didn't want to hurt them. We were a close family, and they had been good to me.

Before I met my wife, I had gone out with quite a few girls. After all, I was twenty-three when I met her. I guess I started dating when I was about fifteen, and by the time I had finished high school there were quite a few girls I had gone with. None of these ventures were at all serious—it was just a matter of going to the movies, going dancing, or something like that. All of these girls were Jewish—I knew them from the neighborhood, or from school, or from some place like that. During this period, I just never went out with a Christian girl. I wouldn't have wanted to, although there was quite a lot of talk among the fellows that they were pretty easy to have a good time with. But even if I had wanted to go out with one, the opportunity wouldn't have presented itself. There just weren't any around, at least not in the circles we moved in. Well, wait a minute. Now that I think of it, I did have a friend who used to go out with a Catholic girl—someone I think he met one summer when he was working in a department store. He used to see a lot of her and he knew a lot of her friends, too. But he never introduced me to any of them. I suppose he felt there'd be no point to it—it would be just like mixing oil and water. . . . After getting out of high school, I was in the army for four years, and for the first time I started meeting Christian girls—at USO dances, around the base, and places like that. Some of them were rather nice, and I dated three or four. But I thought of these relationships as being very temporary. Anyway, I was mostly out for a good time. As far as marriage was concerned, my feelings hadn't changed a bit.

When I got out of the army, I went to college under the G.I.

bill, and I suppose I began to think a little more seriously about marriage. At least I felt it would be nice to go steady with someone, instead of flitting from one girl to the other. Actually, I didn't meet my wife until my junior year, but before that I had what you might call two semi-serious affairs. These were both with Jewish girls, and I guess I should tell you a bit about them. . . . During my freshman year, I had started going to weekly dances that were sponsored by the B'nai B'rith. One night I cut in on this girl (Joan) who was really quite an eye full, and who could chatter away gaily on any subject. She was being given a big rush by all the guys there, but somehow I got the feeling she took a particular shine to me. I remember that every time I cut in on her, she'd give me a big smile and thank me for having saved her from the guy she'd just been dancing with. I suppose I felt kind of flattered. Anyway, after that evening, I saw a good deal of her, and I must say I was kind of stuck on her. But it didn't last very long. I began to wise up to what kind of a girl she *really was*. You see, I had felt that she liked me—you know, really liked me. But the fact is—she had been giving me a big line. All she was interested in was collecting a big string of men, and I was damned if I wanted to be one of her collection. I didn't want to go cavorting about with a gadabout—I wanted someone who was *really* interested in me. . . . As for Sarah—she was the other girl I went with—I met her in New York during summer vacation after my sophomore year. Irving—who was one of my closest friends and with whom I had grown up—had gotten her as a blind date for me one night. When I saw her, I felt he had done all right. She was the type I liked—tall and slender. On that first evening, we all went out bowling, and then we went back to Irving's house and drank beer and danced. She impressed me that first night as being shy and withdrawn— she had a kind of dreamy quality about her. However, after a few more dates, it was apparent she was very intelligent and had a wonderful sense of humor. I saw a lot of her after that— she was good company in a quiet sort of way, and there was no doubt she was really interested in me. However, to make a long story short, I began wondering whether she was emotionally disturbed. There'd been small signs at first, but at the time

I hadn't paid much attention. After all, there's probably no
one who isn't eccentric in some way or other. But after a while,
I began to wonder more and more about her. To give you an
idea of what I mean, Sarah had planned on giving a party, but
the night before she became so overwrought at the prospect of
having it, she called the whole thing off. Another thing—she
was always prudish about necking. At first, she used to put me
off by saying she didn't really know me well enough. When she
finally did agree to neck, she used to stiffen up like a board
and didn't seem to enjoy it at all. I began to think that maybe
she was one of those girls you read about who confess to you
on their wedding night that they feel sex is disgusting. Well,
the whole thing came to an end casually when I went back
to college at the beginning of my junior year. But I couldn't
help feeling I would have saved myself a lot of trouble if I had
only known what Sarah was really like right from the start. In
fact, the same thing might be said of Joan. The thing is—both
of these girls seemed to have such great possibilities at first.

To get around to how I met my wife, in the fall semester of
my junior year at college I took a course in the modern novel. I
had noticed a Jewish girl there for a couple of weeks. (At
that time, I assumed Kay was Jewish: she looked Jewish and
hung around with a girl who I was sure was Jewish.) She had
a good figure and was tall and slender. And she seemed to have
a friendly face; she was always smiling. There was another
thing about her that struck me—she had a very soothing voice.
Some Jewish girls talk in a nasal whine, and I've always been
put off by them. Usually I'm kind of shy about picking up
girls, but in this situation it was easy as pie. During the next
class session, I simply sat down next to her, and before long we
were talking. After class, I asked her if she would like to have
some coffee. Her face lit up, and she said it would be a fine
idea.

That coffee session lasted for about two hours. During that
time, we talked mostly about the course and the different authors we were reading. What impressed me most was that she
seemed to be really absorbed in her work. She was doing a lot
of outside reading on her own—she wanted to know more
about Hemingway, Proust, and the others. It wasn't unknown

for a co-ed to be genuinely interested in her work, but it was at least unusual. There were a lot of girls at college who were just frittering their time away. They were either out to get a little polish, or they were social butterflies. A lot of them were like Joan, who, I remember, used to make a great fetish of the fact that she was getting through without ever having to open a book. Well, Kay was serious about her work. She had a partial scholarship, and after graduation hoped to get a job writing scripts for radio or TV. But while she was serious about her work, she didn't seem to take herself too seriously, if you know what I mean. She could laugh at herself. Aside from these things, I liked the fact that she was a good listener. She seemed anxious to hear what I had to say about the people we were reading. In fact, she seemed interested in anything I had to say. I don't know why, but girls who were good listeners always appealed to me. It's not that I had to be the center of attention. I think I took it as a sign that they wouldn't turn out to be domineering types. Of course, it was also an indication they were interested in me. . . . Before leaving Kay that afternoon, I made a date to meet her a few days later. I felt very pleased about it all. Now that I knew her—at least a little—I felt even more drawn to her than when I had first seen her at a distance in the classroom.

The next time we met, we hadn't been talking for more than ten minutes when I thought she said something about the parochial school she had attended. My first thought was what would a Jewish girl be doing in a parochial school. Then it hit me—she probably wasn't Jewish! At first, I couldn't believe it! The stupid thing was I didn't even know her last name. I hadn't asked for it last time, and she hadn't volunteered it. When I made some half-hearted joke to that effect, she told it to me, and it couldn't be anything but the name of an Italian Catholic. I guess I didn't hear much of what she said during the rest of that coffee date. I felt crestfallen, though I tried not to show it. She had appealed to me a lot more than any girl I had met in some time. I tried to tell myself that it was better I found out now, rather than later, after I had become really stuck on her. After all, I said to myself, she wasn't the only girl on the campus.

During the rest of that semester, I saw Kay occasionally, but

that's about all. As far as my romantic life in general was concerned, it was at a complete standstill. The only girl that caught
my eye was one I never even managed to meet. She was a
Jewish girl—I was sure of that—who I saw in the library. I
used to cook up ways of meeting her, but I never had the nerve
to follow through. Some guys can sidle up to a girl and start a
conversation going, and before you know it the two of them
are walking off somewhere together. I just never seemed to be
able to do that. I needed something to break the ice. With Kay it
had been easy—we were in the same class together, and it was
natural that we should be talking. But here there was nothing
to help me.

At the beginning of the next semester, a notice was posted
on the bulletin board that the dramatic club was going to put on
a musical comedy. The play called for a very large cast and,
according to the notice, tryouts were needed very badly. Anyone who had the slightest interest was begged to show up at
the next meeting. At first, I didn't think anything of it. Then I
thought what the hell, maybe I'll amble over next Saturday and
see what it's all about. In high school I'd been in a few plays,
and it had been fun. More important, life at college was beginning to pall. I was getting tired of sitting in my room studying,
and always being by myself. . . . When I got over to the theater
on Saturday, there were a lot of students sitting around, waiting
for something to happen. I looked around, and then I saw Kay
sitting off to one side with some other people I knew slightly.
I went over and joined them. None of them knew any more than
I did about the play, but they were all very excited and curious.
As it turned out, this whole bunch of us, except for one fellow,
landed small parts in the play. But the really important thing is
that we all became very good friends later. Since this had a lot
to do with what happened between Kay and myself, I should
really tell you more about this group and how it got started. . . .
During the staging of this musical, we used to see a lot of each
other around the theater. There were always rehearsals, and
you had to spend hours waiting around until they got to the
scenes you were in. Well, this bunch of us who met that first
day just seemed to hang around together kind of naturally.
Then, after a while, we got in the habit of going out and having

coffee, or we'd go up to one of the girl's rooms and sit around and talk. I don't know whether you know it or not, but there's something about being in a play that draws people together. There's a lot of excitement, and funny things are always happening. And there's a nervous, jittery feeling when the play is about to open, and you wonder whether you'll get stagefright and mess the whole thing up. Then when it's all over, everyone feels a tremendous sense of relief. All of us had these feelings. We were in the same boat, and just couldn't seem to talk enough about everything that was happening.

After the musical, there were other plays, and we were in many of them together. In time, we became a very close group. I don't know how to describe it. It was the kind of group where we were always ready to go to bat for each other. Let me give you an example. There was this other Jewish boy in the group—his name was Sam—and he looked Jewish from head to toe. Well, Odum, who was the director, seemed to be giving him a raw deal. He always had Sam painting scenery or working the lights, and he just never seemed to have any kind of a part for him. Well, one day Sam asked him what the score was, and Odum told him very sarcastically that as soon as he put on *The Merchant of Venice*, there'd be an excellent spot for him. Sam told me about this a few days later, and I was incensed. The two of us talked it over, but we agreed there wasn't much we could do about it, aside from telling Odum off and not showing up again. As for the other kids, we decided not to say a thing to them. There was really nothing to be gained. Well, we did quit, but the other kids kept badgering us and wanting to know why. Finally, one night Sam told Dot—she was one of the girls in the group—exactly what had happened. I don't know just what occurred after that, but a few days later when we were all together, the whole group just flatly announced they were all going to quit. I was touched, and I'm sure Sam was too. And it took some doing to persuade them not to walk out, but to take the matter to the Dean instead—which they did, incidentally.

Getting back to Kay, naturally I saw quite a lot of her when we were in that first play together and starting to form the same friendships. I tried to keep it innocent and casual and all that—but the fact is she did appeal to me. You couldn't help but like her—she was so excited about the play and so interested in everything that was going on. Then, I guess the fact that everybody else seemed to like her so much made a difference too. These other kids weren't dopes by any means, and they wouldn't have warmed up to anyone who was a pill. It was plain that they thought a lot of her, and I guess that made me like her even more. Still, nothing happened between us until the night the play opened, when there was a big party given for the cast. . . . When I got over to the party that night, there were millions of people milling about, and everybody was feeling very happy. The musical had gone off wonderfully. I looked around and saw Sam reaching for another drink—he already had one in his hand. Before long, we were both kind of tanked and having a fine time. Then—I remember it clearly—he put his hand on my shoulder and said I was a damn fool. He said I should be in the adjoining room dancing with Kay, instead of spending my time getting potted with him. He said he had it on good authority she liked me a lot. I asked him how he got his information, and he told me that Dot had told him. (Dot was one of Kay's roommates.) After another drink, I looked for Kay and asked her to dance. Then after we danced a while and had a few more drinks, we sneaked up into her room in the dorm. She turned the lights off, and in another minute we were sitting on the couch, necking. It all seemed very natural. She was a very passionate girl, and I remember thinking that the guy who married her probably wouldn't be disappointed in bed. She was just nothing like Sarah had been.

After that night, I went out with Kay a few days later and soon we were going around together pretty regularly. As far as the others were concerned, they took our going together for granted. There was never the slightest question of how they felt. They thought it was fine. In fact, Sam was always telling me that, outside of Dot, Kay was one of the nicest girls he had ever met. It was not only that our friends directly encouraged the whole thing. Whether they knew it or not, there were still a lot of other ways in which they were responsible for bringing us closer together. For example, things always seemed to work out so that Kay and I found ourselves together. If we all went off on a ski trip or something like that, it was just taken for granted that Kay and I would ride in the same car. Or if it was my turn to throw a party for the gang, it was assumed, as a matter of course, that Kay would help make the sandwiches, help clean up afterward—be the hostess, in other words. Then too, I learned certain things about Kay, through Dot, that I hadn't really known before. (Kay and I used to double date constantly with Sam and Dot.) For instance, I remember she told me once that it had been Kay who had organized the other kids when that business between Sam and Odum had come up. That was something I hadn't known before. Then again, Dot told me that as far as she knew Kay's religious feelings didn't run very deep—that she probably wouldn't go to mass at all if it weren't for her parents. Certainly, I knew Kay well enough to know she was hardly an ardent Catholic, so that what Dot told me wasn't really a big surprise. I suppose what it did was to confirm what I had suspected. There were also other things about Kay that somehow reached my ears—nice things that couldn't fail to make an impression upon me.

It may seem strange that I kept going with Kay throughout the rest of my stay at college. You see my ideas about marrying a Jewish girl hadn't really changed, at least not during the first year I was going with Kay. I still expected that the girl I married would be Jewish. While it's true that Kay wasn't a doctrinaire Catholic, it's equally true she wasn't a Jew. The thing is—I just never suspected that things would get as serious as they ultimately did. I realized, of course, that I was becoming fonder of Kay all the time, but I would periodically reassure myself that it couldn't possibly go any further. In the last analysis, I guess I felt that I simply wouldn't let myself become more involved. . . . Still, there were many times when I told myself I should really put an end to it. If you're scared of fire, it's best not to play with it. Then too, I felt guilty about monopolizing Kay's time. She was an attractive girl and could have gone out with plenty of other fellows. . . . You know, now that I think of it, I'm sure that our having all of these friends in common had a lot to do with my not breaking off. You see, I'd broken off with other girls in the past—but here the situation was different. Kay and I had all these mutual friends, and we were bound to see a good deal of each other in the future. If I had broken off, it would have been embarrassing as hell. What would we talk about when we met—the weather? Then too, I can imagine how self-conscious I'd have felt if Kay saw me making up to one of the other girls in the group.

All of this went on for about a year—my going with Kay, our having all these friends in common, and all of us being so closely tied up with the theater. Then, something occurred in the middle of my senior year that led me to become even more involved. We had a new dramatic club director then, and this guy picked out Kay and myself to put on a one-act play. The two of us were literally put in charge of the whole shebang. The students submitted original plays, and we had to pick out what we felt was the best; then we had to go ahead and cast it, stage it, direct it, and everything else. Well, as a result of working so closely with Kay, I got an even deeper insight into what kind of a person she really was. Of course, by this time I certainly knew her well—make no mistake about that. But just the same, any dating relationship is apt to be somewhat artificial. You know—you talk, drink beer, go to the movies, dance, neck, etc. Even though this type of thing went on forever, there'd still be a lot of things about the other person you'd never really know about. During the next three months or so, a whole variety of situations came up. I saw how Kay handled them, and it left me with the feeling that I knew her even better than I had before. Let me give you a couple of examples of what I mean: After reading and discussing all of the plays turned in, we both favored one in particular. It was a political satire on McCarthyism—McCarthy and his aides come to the college campus in disguise, they go sleuthing about, and wind up making tremendous jackasses of themselves in the end. At that time, McCarthyism was a very touchy subject, and the director insisted that we clear the play with the Dean. After giving the Dean the play to read, the two of us went to speak with him. He said we were free to go ahead and produce this thing if we wanted to, but he strongly advised us against it. He pointed out that Kay was putting herself in an especially difficult position, since she hoped to work in radio or TV after graduation. As he pointed out, and as we all knew, the entertainment business was very leery of taking on anyone who wasn't "100 per cent

American." And the Dean wasn't the only one who put pressure on us. The Newman Club got wind of it, and they were very upset. Even some of our friends thought we were just sticking our necks out—that we ought to leave well enough alone. Frankly, I began to get nervous about it, and if Kay had wanted to drop it, I'm certain I wouldn't have objected. But she didn't want to drop it at all. She said it was a good play, and that we ought to put it on. She was quite determined, and you couldn't help but admire her mettle. I remember thinking that if Sarah had been in her shoes, she would have folded up like an accordion right after seeing the Dean. She would never have been able to go through with it. As for Joan, I wasn't even sure she had ever heard of McCarthy. I guess this whole episode made me see how much inner strength and self-confidence Kay really had. You couldn't help but realize she was a truly stable person. . . . To give you another example of how I came to know her better, we were choosing a cast for the play when this rather forlorn-looking girl showed up. She was painfully shy, the type who always winds up on the sidelines. While the truth is she had little flair for acting, Kay was anxious that she be given a part. This meant, of course, that Kay would have to spend many extra hours rehearsing her, which she did. What I am trying to get at—there was really no need for her to take all of this upon herself. It wasn't a momentous act, of course, but just the same it was a very kind thing to do. You couldn't help but realize she really cared about other people's feelings. She was a far cry from Joan, for example, who just didn't give a hoot about anyone else.

The play (and it worked out well) was given in May, and we were slated to graduate the next month. After graduation, Kay planned to go home for a few weeks and then come to New York and look for a job. I could hardly wait for her to come to the city—there were so many things I wanted to show her. . . . When I got home after graduation, I started picking up the threads of my life in New York. I saw a lot of my old buddies— particularly Irving, who got me caught up on all the news and gossip in our neighborhood. I wanted to tell him about Kay, but I figured I'd wait a few weeks and surprise him. I was sure that he'd like her. Then, of course, I saw a lot of my folks, since

I lived at home. We used to sit around watching TV in the evening, or sometimes we'd play cards. I told them a lot about my studies in college, and they would kid me all the time about being such a "know-it-all." But they were really very proud of me—my mother was always on the phone spreading the news of my accomplishments. If she wasn't doing that, she'd be in the kitchen cooking something special for me to eat. Ever since I can remember, she has always worried about whether I was eating enough. It was just like old times, when I'd been in high school many years back. There'd just always been a lot of warmth between us. . . .

At this stage, my folks didn't even know that Kay existed. For the last year and a half—that is, ever since I started going with her—I hadn't breathed a word about it to them. For one thing, I just wasn't in the habit of telling them all about my love life. But aside from that, I definitely hadn't wanted them to know. I knew they'd worry about it, and I didn't want to upset them. Why cause them a lot of unnecessary anguish? As I said, I never thought it would really become serious. As I saw it, it was bound to come to nothing in the end. If they *had known* what was going on all the time, it's hard to say what would have happened. Well, to be frank, I think it's very unlikely I would have kept on going with Kay. . . . So, even at this point, I still didn't tell them anything. I dreaded the idea and couldn't face it. Then again, you see, nothing at all had been settled between Kay and me. We certainly hadn't made any plans to get married or anything like that. In fact, we hadn't even ever talked about it. Since everything was still up in the air, there still seemed no reason to bring it all out in the open—at least not then.

At the beginning of July, Kay came to New York, as she had planned. She was terribly excited about the city and wanted to see everything, and for the first few weeks we spent a lot of time tramping all over town. After winding up an afternoon with her, lots of times we would meet the same night. It seemed as though we just couldn't see enough of each other. We went out a lot, too, with Irving and his girl friend. Irving really seemed to warm up to her, and I remember him telling me that I was a lucky guy. I didn't discuss the question of intermarriage or anything like that with him at this time, but I was quite sure he would have thought our getting married was a good idea. Of course, I knew that he'd probably have certain reservations. I knew enough about his background to know that, and I was quite certain he'd never think of intermarrying himself. Still, it was nice to feel that essentially he was behind me. In a way, it was even important, because I was starting to get quite wrought up about the situation at home—or rather what I anticipated the situation would be in the future. You can't help but appreciate your friends at times like this.

Well, while Kay and I were seeing each other during the first month or so, my parents still didn't know anything about it. They knew I was going out a lot, but I let them think I was seeing different girls I had met at college. I'm sure they assumed they were Jewish. . . . Then came a night I won't forget. I had left Kay early. When I got home, my parents weren't watching TV or playing cards—like they usually were. They were sitting on the couch kind of stiffly and their faces seemed drawn. My heart skipped a beat. I was afraid something was up. My mother just sat there, tongue-tied. Finally, my father shouted at her, "So my God, ask him!" My mother wanted to know what it meant that I had been going out with a *shikseh*.* A neighbor of ours, it seems, had seen us out twice and had told my mother about it. I tried to pass it off lightly. I said it was nothing—that Kay was just someone I'd known briefly at college. My mother started sobbing with relief. She said she had known there couldn't have been anything to it. She said I was a good boy and should go to the kitchen and get something to eat. I felt like a lousy hypocrite. But it would have been disastrous if I had suddenly divulged the whole truth. . . . All that night I kept stewing about what I should do. The thing is—I knew I couldn't go on keeping them in the dark forever. They were bound to hear other gossip about Kay and me. But even if they didn't, I still knew I'd have to tell them sometime. I simply couldn't have run off behind their backs and gotten married. It would have killed them. . . . The next few days I kept brooding about what to do. I wanted to think of some way I could get them used to the idea gradually. I felt that they'd take it less badly, if they only learned about it a bit at a time. Finally, I decided it would

* A Gentile girl.

be a good idea if I threw a party at the house and invited Kay, along with a lot of my other friends. This would make it appear casual and innocent-like to my parents. And it would give them a chance to get to know her a little. I knew they would like her. Rather, I knew they would like her as long as they didn't suspect I was serious. At any rate, I planned to have the party the following week.

Once I had decided on a definite course of action, I felt a lot better. But it didn't last very long. I started to become more and more tense and worked up. I couldn't seem to get hold of myself —I couldn't sleep, I couldn't concentrate, I couldn't get my mind off my parents. I just couldn't bear to face the whole issue that would inevitably come up between us. I kept putting the party off, and it was three months before I got up the nerve to go through with it. . . . During this period, I continued to see a great deal of Kay. Somehow, I was always pouring my heart out to her. I told her all about my parents and how they felt. Mostly she would just listen and try to understand. Then too, I would talk a lot about what I was going through. The thing is— she was always so understanding. Just being with her always made me feel a lot better. If she had acted any differently, I just don't see how I could have kept on going. I don't know how to put it, except that she was always there when I needed her, and I needed her very badly during this period. . . . As I look back now, I think I fell even more deeply in love with her during those months when I was having such a difficult time. I guess I couldn't help but realize just how much she really loved me. . . .

Along about midnight on the night of the party, Kay and a few others lingered on after the others had left. Kay had met my folks briefly earlier, but there had been a lot of people milling about, and no chance to talk. Later we all just sat around in the living room. From what I could gather, Kay was making a good impression—although she had only been making small talk like the rest. However, I hoped my parents might get some inkling of what she was really like, so I steered the conversation into other channels. I got Kay to describe her role in putting on the McCarthy play, and how she had stood up to the Dean and a lot of others. My father had always admired people with strength and conviction. Well, she told the whole story—although I wished she hadn't been so modest about it. At any rate, my folks seemed to be impressed, and they kept nodding their heads as she talked. After that, the conversation moved to other topics, and I wasn't able to steer it back to Kay in a way that wouldn't have been too conspicuous. . . . After I returned home that night, after seeing Kay home, the lights were on, and my folks were still up. They looked very worried, but didn't say anything. Then, my mother finally said, "That's a nice girl. She should marry some nice Catholic boy." I told them I thought she was nice, too; and that I had recently seen her a number of times. Then, suddenly the strain of the previous months told on me. What the hell, I thought, get it over with! "Who knows," I said, "I might even marry her myself someday." My father didn't say a word, but my mother burst into tears and became hysterical.

They took it worse than I had ever imagined they would. During the next ten days my mother was hysterical much of the time. Their arguments were endless: How could I turn my back on everything they had taught me! How could I be so ungrateful! I was breaking their hearts! Their only son was making a laughing stock out of them! They didn't have very nice things to say about Kay either: she was common, she'd wear the pants in the family, she had fancy ideas about being a writer and wouldn't stay at home! They said her parents were probably Nazis and would spit on me. Our children would be bastardized and would turn against me. It was impossible to reason with them—they were so emotional. I didn't say much except that nothing had been settled between Kay and myself and I needed more time to think it over. I should add that my parents weren't the only ones who were upset. As soon as my uncle heard about it, he came over to the house right away. He said that mixed marriages never worked out, and that I would die of shame if I betrayed the Jews. My aunt in Chicago wrote me a letter, begging me not to do this to the family. This whole period was a nightmare, but this was just the beginning: About two weeks after my parents found out, I went over to see Irving one evening. I hadn't seen him since the night of the party, because he'd been out of town. I told him about everything that had happened. I expected him to back me up as I talked, but he just sat there, very quiet. Finally, I pressed him and asked what he would do if he were in my position. He still didn't say much. He just said you have to consider your parents in a thing like this, and that my uncle was probably right—mixed marriages are a very risky business. I can't say I was surprised by his reservations. But I was taken aback that he didn't say more. You see, I had been convinced that essentially he would back me up in this thing. I had gone on believing he was behind me a lot more than he actually was. (A couple of years later, and quite accidently, I learned how Irving had really felt at this point. He was wholeheartedly against it and "couldn't see what I saw in that girl anyway.") . . . After leaving his house early that evening, I ambled through the streets in a kind of daze. I felt terribly unsettled—the supports had been knocked out from under me. When I finally got home, my parents were still up. Something seemed to be different. Then, my father came over to me and said there would be no more words between us about this thing. Now it was all up to me. But if I married Kay, they would never set foot in our house as long as they lived.

The next morning I called Kay and said I had to see her. When I got there, I told her I couldn't go on, and that this would have to be the end.

On the same afternoon I packed my clothes and other belongings and moved out. I told my folks it was all over between Kay and me, and that I was moving out because I wanted to be by myself for a while. I felt I had to get away from them. I took a room in another part of town, and for the first time in months I relaxed. This whole thing had been preying on my mind for so long, that when I finally settled it, it was like having a great weight removed from my chest. . . . Inevitably, my euphoria wore off, and I began to feel more and more lonely. Everything kept reminding me of Kay. . . . I determined to keep busy—I spent a lot of time studying and going to the movies. But mostly I made an effort to see as many people as I could. I hung out a lot with Irving and my other friends—all of whom seemed determined to get me back into the swing of things. For example, if we were at a party, they always had someone they wanted me to meet. A few of these girls—I don't deny it—were attractive, but I couldn't make the effort to get to know them. I just wasn't up to making small talk with strangers, to starting all over again with someone new. I began wondering about some of the girls I used to run around with. I don't know why, but I had a yen to see them. I asked Irving, I remember, what had become of Sarah. He told me she was going steady with some kid I had known in school. It was the same with all the others—they were either going steady, had gotten married, or had moved out of the neighborhood. Time hadn't stood still during the years I had been going with Kay. Life had been going on without me. For all the contacts I had, I might as well have been living in Shanghai!

During this period, I had plenty of time to think about my parents. While all the fireworks had been going on, I had felt kind of numbed. Now I had a lot of time to think, and a lot of buried feelings began coming to the surface, particularly feelings of resentment. The fact that they had so blatantly intervened between Kay and myself angered me. What right did they have to decide my life for me? Whose business was it who I married anyway—theirs or mine? I began to boil when I thought of how they had acted. There was something else, too, that incensed me: My parents had kept harping on things that just didn't seem very important—how would they get on with Kay's folks, what would happen when the family had a *Seder?* * Maybe they wouldn't get on with Kay's folks, and maybe Kay and I would never be invited to a family *Seder!* But why the hell was it so important? The thing is that I was in love with Kay, and she was in love with me. This never seemed to cut much ice with them. When I tried to impress them with our love, they would just shrug it off. My mother would say, "So much talk about love! So is this Hollywood? You can only think about love!" The fact of the matter is that their standards were not mine, and I became angered at the thought of their imposing their values on me. There's another thing too. I used to have the same daydream over and over again: I would see my parents, in my mind's eye, kicking up a big fuss no matter who I wanted to marry. They didn't want me ever to leave them and have a life of my own. They just wanted to hold on to me, rather than face the prospect of being lonely in their old age. Feelings of

* The yearly dinner to commemorate the Jews' escape from Egypt.

resentment would well up in me as I pictured them selfishly
using me for their own ends. I don't know if I really believed in
these daydreams—I guess I did. I guess I half convinced myself
that my parents would really act this way. . . . I always felt a lot
better after going through these orgies of resentment. I began
to feel that it was actually my parents who were at fault and
not me. I began to see myself in a new light. Maybe I wasn't
such a heel after all just because I wanted to marry the girl I
loved. . . .

Also, I would often wonder what would really happen if I did
go ahead and marry Kay. I began to question whether my parents would really disown me. Maybe they hadn't really meant
what they'd said, or maybe they'd change their minds. Being an
only child does make a difference. They'd be grief-stricken
about losing me, and I wasn't at all sure they were prepared to
make that kind of sacrifice. I know when we had fights before,
they'd always managed to come around. Of course, this was
different—but it does make a difference when you're the only
child in the family. Then, too, I thought they might become less
hostile if Kay agreed to see things my way, religiously speaking.
It's true that when I had brought this up before, it never seemed
to make a dent in my mother's armor. When I told her Kay was
willing to convert (although I didn't actually think Kay would
be willing to go that far), my mother always responded with
contempt. She said if Kay were any kind of a girl, she'd stand
up for her own religion and not go around pretending she was
a Jew. Despite what she said, I still felt it might make a difference if Kay would see things my way.

About six weeks after our break-up, I went back to college
for a few days to visit Sam. I had written him about everything
that had happened, and he had been after me for some time to
come up for a visit. I was anxious to see him. I felt it would
help get my mind off Kay, my parents, and everything else. The
night I arrived we went out to drink beer at the tavern, and
before long we were reminiscing about the kids we had known
at college and the good times we had all had together. I told
him this had been the happiest time of my life. Before I knew it,
I was telling him again about everything that had happened
between Kay and me. For a while, he just sat there and listened.

Then, after a few more beers, he said there'd been something on his mind he'd been wanting to say for a long time. In a nutshell, he felt I was acting like a damn fool. How could I be so crazy as to give up a girl like Kay! Who was marrying her anyway, he wanted to know, me or my parents? So what if our religions were different? Other people had made a go of mixed marriages! He was convinced I was making a big mistake, and that it would be insane of me to give her up. After everyone had been against me for so long, it gave me a wonderful feeling to hear what he said. Of course, don't misunderstand me—I wasn't surprised by what he said. We were close friends, and I had always known how he felt about Kay and me. In fact, he had talked her up before I really started going with her. There was no chance of his turning out to be another Irving—someone who was just putting on an act. . . . Going home on the train the next day, I kept thinking about all the things Sam had said. Somehow I felt closer to him than I ever had before. The train seemed to make a million stops. When it finally got in, I ran across the station and dialed Kay's number.

As you can imagine, my calling Kay constituted a turning point in our affair. I've wondered, more than once, what made me do it. I would say that there were three things involved. In the first place, my parents being so against it just didn't seem to weigh on me so heavily any more. As I told you, I became more and more resentful toward them and began to shift the blame onto their shoulders a lot more. At the same time, I began to feel that even though I did go through with this thing, they might still come around in the end. Secondly, there was Sam who gave me a push at just the right time. But there was also something else that only gradually became clear to me. As I mentioned, all of the girls I was meeting during our break were new to me, and I just couldn't make the effort to get to know them. The fact is—I just didn't have any real ties with anyone else. And it was this, I would say, that indirectly drove me back to Kay. To be frank with you, I don't know what would have happened if I had kept a couple of reserve girl friends in cold storage. If you think about it, when the hero breaks off with his girl friend in the movies, there's always an "old faithful" who's been waiting for him to return. He scurries back to her, she greets him with open arms, and his troubles are over. In my case, not only was there no "old faithful"—I knew hardly any girls at all. It was this feeling of bleakness, of being so alone, that made me want to be back with Kay more than ever. Yet, what's even stranger about all this is that I had brought the whole situation upon myself! You see, after I started going with Kay, I made little effort to keep up my old contacts, and the thought of looking for new ones never occurred to me. For example, there wasn't a single thing to prevent my going to the weekly dances given by the B'nai B'rith—but the thought of doing it didn't enter my mind. My friends never thought of introducing me to anyone new either, at least I don't think they did. It wouldn't have occurred to them, because as far as they were concerned, I was hooked. If you come right down to it—and it's ironic—my being so out of touch was no one's doing but my own!

To get back to Kay and me, a few days later we took up the question of the children. At first, Kay felt there was no point in trying to decide it now—that it would be better to wait and see. But if we had to decide it right away, she felt some in-between religion like Ethical Culture might be a good idea. After I kept insisting that this wouldn't provide any kind of a real solution, she finally gave in and agreed to raise them as Jewish. As for raising them as Catholics, the subject was never brought up. She probably knew how I would have reacted. About the ceremony, I was anxious to be married by a rabbi— not only for my sake, but particularly for the sake of my parents. Well, in the end, Kay agreed to a Jewish wedding. Soon after, we found a rabbi who would marry us, and we set a date to be married. . . . It's funny, but we had never really talked about these things before. I suppose it's something you don't talk about unless you're seriously thinking about marriage. Just the same, I'd always suspected that Kay would go along with me in these matters. As a matter of fact, this may help explain why I initially fell for her. I mean, if she'd been the same girl—but an ardent Catholic—I don't know that all this would have happened. . . . You'd have to speak to Kay to really find out just why she did go along with me. But, basically, I think she understood how much the whole thing really meant to me. You know, I was thinking—if it turned out that she had felt as strongly as I did, it would be pretty hard to say what would have happened. But if I had to guess, I suspect she still would have given in. You see, as much as I needed her, I have the feeling she needed me even more. It's possible she would have given in on this thing for the sake of getting married. . . . There's something else I should mention. When mixed couples, like Kay and myself, come to decide these matters, the whole thing is left pretty much up to them. Of course, members of the family as well as rabbis, priests, and others will have strong feelings—but that isn't at all what I mean. What I mean is there's no general feeling from the outside that the children should be raised one way or the other, or that either Kay or I should have more say in the matter. Everything is left pretty much up in the air. Well, in a sense, this vagueness played right into my hands. It all boiled down to which of us felt more strongly. And since I felt more strongly—there was really nothing to stop me from having my own way. I don't mean I didn't ever have qualms about being kind of high-handed. After all, Kay had as much justification for raising the children as Catholics as I did for raising them as Jews. In fact, some people would say she had more justification, since she would be their mother. Well, these things bothered me some—but certainly not enough to make me act any differently than I did.

Aside from the religious angle, there was another problem about our children that ran through my mind. I wanted others to think of them as Jewish, not just in a religious sense, but in a social sense, if you know what I mean. This may sound strange to you, because being Jewish isn't exactly a bed of roses when it comes to getting jobs, getting into college, and things like that. But since the Jews are pushed down—whether I happen to like it or not—I didn't want to see my children running away from it. I wanted them to face up to it, to be thought of as full-time Jews. You may wonder what I had to worry about, since Kay had agreed to give them Jewish training. Well, let me give you an example. You've probably run into children of mixed parentage who are being raised as Christians, but who people look on as not being *really* Christian. Well, I didn't want to have the reverse situation happen to me. But there were a couple of reasons why I wasn't really worried. For one thing, it seems to me that people usually take more account of who the child's father is than who his mother is. But even if this weren't the case, some people believe that any Jewish blood—whether the mother's or father's—automatically makes the children Jewish. I felt that both of these factors stacked the cards in my favor, that is, it would be very unlikely that our children would ever be viewed as anything but Jewish. To be accurate about this whole thing, I should add that I never explicitly thought all this out. All of this just passed through my mind, if you know what I mean.

If Kay had held out for some other religious solution, I don't really know what would have happened. But the fact that she did see things my way certainly made everything easier. Her being a Christian just didn't bother me so much any more. I felt it would help with my parents too. And I turned out to be right—at least they came to the wedding.

The processes responsible for the subject's marriage are "condensed" below. These can be grouped around eight main points:

1. Our subject was attracted to his future wife immediately because of certain features which were observable (she was physically appealing; she had a pleasant voice). Moreover, the external setting facilitated their meeting (they were in the same class).

2. He was not aware of her ethnic affiliation at the time of their introduction. If he had been, he wouldn't have asked her out for coffee and thereby discerned other pleasing things about her (she was interested in her work, she listened to him, etc.)

3. She was superior to his ingroup dating partners in ways which were *vitally important* to him:

    a) She possessed a number of "objective" assets—although these were *not* immediately perceivable (she had strength of character; she was kind; she was sexually responsive,* etc.). The external setting was instrumental in bringing certain of these assets into view. For purposes of analysis, three external settings, each of which played a role in this process, can be delineated:

(1) The dramatic club, in which they were both active members, encouraged their interaction.

(2) Their network of mutual friends performed the same function, both intentionally and unintentionally.

(3) Their assignment to work together (to produce a play) forced them to interact.

b) After she got to know our subject, the girl was very responsive, and probably more so than his previous dating partners who had been Jewish. Moreover, at a later period, her responsiveness came at a time when it was especially appreciated—when he was undergoing a great deal of stress at the prospect of facing his parents.

4. Despite the fact that he had become interested in her, our subject felt sure that he would not become deeply involved emotionally. For this reason, in conjunction with others, he continued to see her. His decision to continue the relationship led to the following consequences: He recognized more fully what she was like beneath the surface, and he became increasingly cut off from other marital prospects. As a result, he became both more attached and more dependent on her.

5. The girl made certain religious concessions: She agreed to be married by a rabbi and to raise their children

* To avoid any misunderstanding, we are referring to the fact that she was *capable* of being sexually responsive, in contrast to women who are inhibited or even frigid.

as Jews. Her acquiescence stemmed from the fact that, of the two, she was less committed to her faith; and perhaps also from the fact that she was more involved emotionally and therefore more willing to make such sacrifices. In addition, our subject's "victory" was promoted by the "neutrality" of the social structure, which does not constrain mixed couples to choose one religion rather than the other or place greater authority in the hands of either sex with respect to this decision. Since our subject felt more strongly about his faith, there was nothing, structurally speaking, to prevent him from having his own way.

Aside from the religious aspect, *per se,* our subject was concerned about how his children would be regarded by others. He realized that the outcome would be determined partly by the social structure, and in a way which was to his advantage. Since he was a male and Jewish, he felt confident that his children would be regarded as Jewish.

6. The image which the subject's parents had of the affair failed to keep abreast of its actual course. When their son was at college, his parents were wholly unaware of the relationship; furthermore, when they did learn of its existence, they underestimated its seriousness for some time. Had their perception not lagged, they would have brought pressure to bear sooner, and our subject might have attempted to terminate the relationship at an earlier stage. Under these circumstances, it is less likely the two would have reunited, because their feelings for each other were less intense at this point.

7. A number of conditions served to insulate this Reluctant from the pressure brought to bear by his parents: He felt their intervention, as well as the substance of their objections, was morally offensive; he was exposed to their protests less frequently because he moved away from home; finally, he felt his parents might become more accepting,

either "on their own" or because of special steps he would take. As a result, his parents' feelings carried less weight.

8. Because of the cross-pressures to which the subject was exposed—he was drawn to his partner, and at the same time he wished to retreat—the reactions of his friends took on added importance.

Let us examine the behavior of his two close friends. In terms of real feelings, Irving disapproved of the relationship to the same degree that Sam approved of it. However, our subject was not equally aware of how they felt: Irving inhibited the expression of his feelings; Sam very definitely did not. Consequently, the composite influence on the subject, insofar as his friends were concerned, was skewed toward the positive pole.

At this point there are a number of things to be said about the influences itemized above and the study as a whole. To begin with, we do not wish to imply that all of the factors described above must be present before an ethnic Reluctant will marry out of his group. The mere presence of certain conditions may be sufficient to account for the act. For example, if the Reluctant feels that his partner is both outstanding and unique, a marriage may occur despite the efforts of parents and friends to prevent it. Conversely, even though all the factors noted may be present, a marriage is not inevitable. The Reluctant may require additional facilitants, in order to make this decision; indeed, he may not marry out of his ethnic group under any conditions.*

Secondly, one "influence," which has been the object of much attention in the professional literature, has scarcely been touched on in this study. We are referring to "attitude

---

* Obviously, psychological factors can be of great importance in explaining such marriages. It is just as obvious, we hope, that we neglected to consider such factors, not because we prejudged them to be irrelevant, but because our perspective has been sociological.[1]

change," in the restricted sense of a change in attitude in one individual toward some given dimension of another individual.* To place this variable within the framework of our study, let us consider the Reluctant whose resistance toward intermarriage stems wholly from his personal feelings, that is, whose resistance is independent of the disapproval of his parents and others. As he sees more of his partner, he may become more tolerant of her affiliation and, in general, of the outgroup of which she is a member. The fact that she is Jewish or Christian no longer makes as much difference (quite apart from any religious concessions she may make). While we do not know whether the Reluctants in our group underwent such "attitude changes," increased tolerance may be of considerable importance in explaining why relationships of this type develop. At the same time, there is an apparently widespread opinion that such relationships cannot develop unless A does, in fact, become more accepting of B's disability (whatever it may be); and that if he does become more accepting, no other influences need be considered. It is our own opinion that both of these beliefs are in error; in a sense, our study has attempted to demonstrate this.

Finally, we would remind the reader of the tentative nature of our findings. Pertinent data were often lacking. In a sense this was inevitable, because many of the topics with which we were concerned grew out of the interviews themselves. That is, it was the respondents' disclosures which first stimulated our interest in these topics, and then led us to reflect further upon them. However, since many of the individuals we had interviewed previously had not addressed themselves to these topics, we found ourselves with gaps in the data, technically speaking. In addition,

---

* The term "attitude change," as used by social scientists, is apt to be assigned different meanings. Sometimes the actor's attitude toward a *certain dimension* of the other person changes; sometimes his attitude toward the other as a *total person* changes. It is useful, at least for our purposes, to keep these two meanings distinct.

the fact that we were unable to contact Reluctants who had been emotionally involved with cross-ethnics, but who later terminated their relationship, has handicapped us at every point. The lack of a control group has prevented us from detecting the presence of certain influences and, quite possibly, has led us to assign undue weight to others. For these reasons (plus the fact that the small size of our "sample" has restricted the range of influences which could be identified), our study must be considered only a first and preliminary step in the research in this area.

Viewed in a broader perspective, intermarriage on the part of ethnic Reluctants is merely one instance of a general phenomenon. Clearly, there are any number of other occasions when individuals become drawn to "ineligibles." Marriages which were previously considered "out of the question," whatever the reasons, occur every day. Or the issue may involve friendship, rather than marriage. A "liberal" Northerner befriends a "traditional" Southerner; a political reformer befriends a "crooked" politician; a resentful step-child becomes attached to a "hateful" stepmother. Such occurrences are legion.

Inevitably, the question arises as to whether the processes which lead to intermarriage will lead to other relationships of this general type. While the answer will depend upon the results of future research along these lines, one of our basic assumptions has been that these relationships are parallel, at least to some extent, in that the factors which facilitate one will also facilitate the others. This assumption, in effect, has provided a major rationale for our study: By focusing on one instance of this phenomenon, we hoped to shed some light on others.

Of course, as one moves from category to category, so to speak, certain differences will inevitably emerge. Marriages and friendships are not identical phenomena, nor are the processes which promote or deter them. Nor will an individual's resistance to befriending or marrying an ineligible invariably derive from the same source. One person's reluctance may stem from "personal" feelings; another's may reflect his fear of the disapproval of others (and these others need not necessarily be parents or friends). If, in both instances, these individuals are drawn to an ineligible, despite their resistance, we would expect the influences responsible to differ to some extent.

Moreover, the barriers which separate different sets of individuals are not equally susceptible to modification. For example, let us suppose that the individual's "disability" resides in his having offensive aspirations or the "wrong" religion. He is in a position to alter this so-called disability, if he so desires. And, in all probability, his accommodation to the other person will further the relationship. On the other hand, certain disqualifying features, such as the color of one's skin, one's age, or the fact that one has a prison record cannot be eradicated. In these instances the actor is unable to appease the other, and if the other does not become more tolerant of the disability in question, the barrier which separates the two will persist. Under such conditions—that is, when the barrier is structurally unmodifiable and the other person does not become more accepting—we can safely conclude that additional facilitants will be required if an affective relationship is to develop.*

While the influences which lead to intermarriage will differ from those which lead to other "tabooed" relationships, it is likely that some of the same causal factors will obtain. In the preceding review of our findings, we enumerated some of these factors. However, at this point, it may

---

* A structurally unmodifiable barrier precludes what has been termed an "alloplastic" adjustment: "One makes an alloplastic adjustment when he attempts to express his wishes by modifying the environment. . . . One makes an autoplastic adjustment when he modifies his own wishes in order to bring them into line with the environmental possibilities as conceived of by himself."[2]

be helpful if we present our findings in the form of some general questions, which might serve as a guide for future inquiries. For purposes of illustration, let us consider a situation in which an individual (whom we shall call A) meets an ineligible (B). We are interested in whether they will establish an intimate relationship and, more specifically, in the factors which might lead to this result.

1. Whatever the nature of B's disability, will A be unaware of its presence initially?

If yes, will the relationship be retarded less than might otherwise be the case?

2. Will B possess certain compensating features (either "objective" characteristics or ways of responding to A)?

If yes, will these features be immediately observable, with the result that A will be aware of their presence from the start? If they are non-observable initially, will the conditions surrounding the relationship enable A to discern their presence eventually?

3. Once A begins to feel kindly disposed toward B, will he feel confident that the two will not become closer, that the relationship will not present a "problem"?

If yes, will this lead A to continue to associate with B? And will the fact that A continues to associate with B directly and/or indirectly lead him to become more attached to B?

4. Is B's disability capable of being altered?

If yes, will B be willing to alter it? If B does accommodate A, will this promote the relationship?

5. Will those who disapprove of the relationship fail to keep abreast of its development, and thus fail to deter its progress?

6. Even if they are aware of its development, will those who are opposed to the relationship conceal their disapproval or at least refrain from actively intervening?

7. Will any conditions be present which will insulate A from whatever negative pressure is brought to bear?

8. For the reasons above (or others), will the deterring influence of those who disapprove of the relationship be weaker than the facilitating influence of those who approve of it?

There is much to be learned about such relationships— both with regard to the processes responsible for their formation and the conditions under which they develop. Clearly, it is knowledge worth having, for such relationships may lead to new associational patterns—associational patterns which will have a profound effect upon our society in the future.

Reference Notes

CHAPTER 1

1. For data as to where married couples first met, see Ernest W. Burgess and Harvey J. Locke, *The Family*, 2nd ed. (New York: American Book, 1953), pp. 353–54; and Paul Popenoe, cited in Willard Waller, *The Family*, revised by Reuben Hill (New York: Dryden, 1951), p. 206.

2. Donald M. Marvin, "Occupational Propinquity as a Factor in Marriage Selection," *Publications of the American Statistical Association*, Vol. 16 (1918–1919), pp. 131–50.

3. For a review of the many studies dealing with the role of residential propinquity in mate selection, see Alvin M. Katz and Reuben Hill, "Residential Propinquity and Marital Selection: A Review of Theory, Method, and Fact," *Marriage and Family Living*, Vol. 20 (February 1958), pp. 27–35.

4. Romanzo Adams, *Interracial Marriage in Hawaii* (New York: Macmillan, 1937), p. 191.

5. Kurt B. Mayer, *The Population of Switzerland* (New York: Columbia University Press, 1952), pp. 184–86. Similar findings have been reported for the United States and Canada (Harvey J. Locke, Georges Sabagh, and Mary M. Thomas, "Interfaith Marriages," *Social Problems*, Vol. 4 [April 1957], pp. 329–33).

6. Louis Rosenberg, *Canada's Jews* (Montreal: Canadian Jewish Congress, 1939), p. 106.

7. Uriah Z. Engelman, "Intermarriage Among Jews in Germany, U.S.S.R., and Switzerland," *Jewish Social Studies*, Vol. 2 (April 1940), pp. 157–78.

8. There have been a number of empirical attempts to discover just what young people look for in their mates. See, for example, Ray E. Baber, *Marriage and the Family* (New York: McGraw-Hill, 1939), pp. 147–51; Harold T. Christensen, *Marriage Analysis* (New York: Ronald Press, 1950), pp. 255–57; Mirra Komarovsky, "What Do Young People Want in a Marriage Partner?" *Journal of Social Hygiene* (December 1946), pp. 2–6; Judson T. Landis and Mary G. Landis, *Building a Successful Marriage* (New York: Prentice-Hall, 1953), pp. 82–87. Rich qualitative interview material bearing upon this subject can be found in Anselm Strauss, *A Study of Three Psychological Factors Affecting Choice of Mate in a College Metropolitan Population* (Ph.D. dissertation, University of Chicago, 1945).

9. See, for example, J. C. Flügel, *The Psychoanalytic Study of the Family* (London: Hogarth, 1950), Chaps. 2, 3, 11.

10. Robert F. Winch, *The Modern Family* (New York: Henry Holt, 1952), p. 406.

11. *Ibid.*, p. 411. A number of efforts have been made to test this theory: e.g., Robert F. Winch, Thomas Ktsanes, and Virginia Ktsanes, "The Theory of Complementary Needs in Mate Selection: An Analytic and Descriptive Study," *American Sociological Review,* Vol. 19 (June 1954) pp. 241–49; Robert F. Winch, "The Theory of Complementariness," *American Sociological Review,* Vol. 20 (February 1955), pp. 52–56; Robert F. Winch, "The Theory of Complementary Needs in Mate Selection: Final Results on the Test of the General Hypothesis," *American Sociological Review,* Vol. 20 (October 1955), pp. 552–55. A more recent exposition of the theory can be found in Robert F. Winch, *Mate-Selection* (New York: Harper, 1958).

12. *Human Society* (New York: Macmillan, 1949), p. 149.

13. Ernest W. Burgess and Paul Wallin, *Engagement and Marriage* (Chicago: Lippincott, 1953), p. 289. (The figures were tabulated from data provided.) The disapproval of friends is also associated with broken engagements (*ibid.*, p. 563). For further evidence that parents influence their children's marital decisions, see Alan Bates, "Parental Roles in Courtship," *Social Forces,* Vol. 20 (May 1942), pp. 483–86; Marvin B. Sussman, "Parental Participation in Mate Selection and Its Effect upon Family Continuity," *Social Forces,* Vol. 32 (October 1953), pp. 76–81.

14. Waller, *op. cit.,* Chaps. 6–12. See, also, the recently completed study by Charles D. Bolton: *The Development Process in Love Relationships* (Ph.D. dissertation, University of Chicago, 1959).

15. See, for example, Stuart W. Cook and Claire Selltiz, "Some Factors Which Influence the Attitudinal Outcomes of Personal Contact," *International Social Science Bulletin,* Vol. 7 (1955), pp. 51–58; George C. Homans, *The Human Group* (New York: Harcourt, Brace, 1950); Paul F. Lazarsfeld and Robert K. Merton, "Friendship as Social Process: A Substantive and Methodological Analysis," in Morroe Berger, Theodore Abel, and Charles H. Page (eds.), *Freedom and Control in Modern Society* (Toronto: Van Nostrand, 1954), pp. 18–66; Theodore M. Newcomb, "The Prediction of Interpersonal Attraction," *The American Psychologist,* Vol. 11 (November 1956), pp. 575–86; Edward A. Suchman, John P. Dean, and Robin M. Williams, Jr., *Desegregation: Some Propositions and Research Suggestions* (New York: Anti-Defamation League of B'nai B'rith, 1958); Robin M. Williams, Jr., "Continuity and Change in Sociological Study," *American Sociological Review,* Vol. 23 (December 1958), pp. 619–33.

CHAPTER 2

1. John E. Mayer, *Jewish-Gentile Intermarriage in the U.S.* (M.A. thesis, Columbia University, Department of Sociology, 1951).

2. For the historical position of various religious groups toward intermarriage and for an extensive bibliography of the literature dealing with intermarriage, see Milton L. Barron, *People Who Intermarry* (Syracuse: Syracuse University Press, 1946).

3. The contemporary outlook and policies of various churches toward interfaith marriages are reported in James H. S. Bossard and Eleanor S. Boll, *One Marriage Two Faiths* (New York: Ronald Press, 1957), Chap. 5; and James A. Pike, *If You Marry Outside Your Faith* (New York: Harper, 1954), Chaps. 5, 6.

4. Marshall Sklare and Marc Vosk, *The Riverton Study* (The American Jewish Committee, 1957), p. 35.

5. "The Fortune Survey," *Fortune Magazine* (November 1942), p. 10.

6. For intermarriage rates in American cities, see Nathan Goldberg, "The Jewish Population in the United States," in *The Jewish People, Past and Present*, Vol. 2 (New York: Jewish Encyclopedic Handbooks, 1948), pp. 25–34; Hershel Shanks, "Jewish-Gentile Intermarriage: Facts and Trends." *Commentary* (October 1953), pp. 370–75. Attention should also be called to a recent survey of Washington, D.C., which has relatively complete intermarriage coverage and various kinds of breakdowns. (See Stanley K. Bigman, *The Jewish Population of Greater Washington in 1956* [Washington: The Jewish Community Council of Greater Washington, 1957], Chap. 8).

7. *Current Population Reports*, Series P–20, No. 79, Table 6.

8. J. S. Slotkin, "Jewish-Gentile Intermarriage in Chicago," *American Sociological Review*, Vol. 7 (February 1942), pp. 34–39.

9. St. Clair Drake and Horace R. Cayton, *Black Metropolis* (New York: Harcourt, Brace, 1945), p. 148. For other instances where, seemingly, intermarried respondents were not averse to crossing group lines in marriage, see Linton C. Freeman, "Homogamy in Interethnic Mate Selection," *Sociology and Social Research*, Vol. 39 (July–August 1955), pp. 369–77; Chester L. Hunt and Richard W. Coller, "Intermarriage and Cultural Change: A Study of Philippine-American Marriages," *Social Forces*, Vol. 35 (March 1957), pp. 223–30. For a recent study which compares the background characteristics of those who contracted a religious intermarriage with those who married someone of the same religion, see Jerold S. Heiss, "Premarital Characteristics of the Religiously Intermarried in an Urban Area," *American Sociological Review*, Vol. 25 (February 1960), pp. 47–55.

10. See, for example, Uriah Z. Engelman, "Intermarriage Among Jews in Germany, U.S.S.R., and Switzerland," *Jewish Social Studies*, Vol. 2 (April 1940), pp. 157–78; Arthur Ruppin, *The Jewish Fate and Future* (London: Macmillan, 1940), pp. 105–15. For an attempt to relate this phenomenon to anti-Semitism within a society, see John E. Mayer, "Jewish-Gentile Intermarriage Patterns: A Hypothesis," *Sociology and Social Research*, Vol. 45 (January 1961), pp. 188–95.

11. George E. Simpson and J. Milton Yinger, *Racial and Cultural Minorities*, rev. ed. (New York: Harper, 1958), pp. 677–80.

12. On this point, see Melvin L. Kohn and Robin M. Williams, Jr., "Situational Patterning in Intergroup Relations," *American Sociological Review*, Vol. 21 (April 1956), pp. 164–74.

CHAPTER 3

1. Paul F. Lazarsfeld and Robert K. Merton, "Friendship as Social Process: A Substantive and Methodological Analysis," in Morroe Berger,

Theodore Abel, and Charles H. Page, (eds.), *Freedom and Control in Modern Society* (Toronto: Van Nostrand, 1954), p. 32.

2. Gordon W. Allport and Bernard M. Kramer, "Some Roots of Prejudice," *Journal of Psychology,* Vol. 22 (1946), p. 17.

CHAPTER 4

1. See, for example, Joseph Golden, "Characteristics of the Negro-White Intermarried in Philadelphia," *American Sociological Review,* Vol. 18 (April 1953), pp. 177–83; Robert K. Merton, "Intermarriage and the Social Structure: Fact and Theory," *Psychiatry,* Vol. 4 (August 1941), pp. 361–74; Louis Wirth and Herbert Goldhamer, "The Hybrid and the Problem of Miscegenation," in Otto Klineberg (ed.), *Characteristics of the American Negro* (New York: Harper, 1944), Part 5, Chap. 4.

2. Kingsley Davis, "Intermarriage in Caste Societies," *American Anthropologist,* Vol. 43 (July–September 1941), pp. 376–95.

3. Ernest W. Burgess and Paul Wallin, *Engagement and Marriage* (Chicago: Lippincott, 1953), p. 211.

4. Eli Ginzberg, *et. al., Occupational Choice* (New York: Columbia University Press, 1951), p. 27.

5. These items, selected solely for purposes of illustration, were drawn from Ray E. Baber, *Marriage and the Family* (New York: McGraw-Hill, 1939), p. 149; Harold T. Christensen, *Marriage Analysis* (New York: Ronald Press, 1950), p. 256; Mirra Komarovsky, "What Do Young People Want in a Marriage Partner," *Journal of Social Hygiene* (December 1946), p. 6; Judson T. Landis and Mary G. Landis, *Building a Successful Marriage* (New York: Prentice-Hall, 1953), p. 84.

6. Christensen, *op. cit.*

7. Manford H. Kuhn, "The Engagement: Thinking about Marriage," in Howard Becker and Reuben Hill, *Family, Marriage, and Parenthood* (Boston: Heath, 1948), p. 293.

8. For a penetrating analysis of the problems individuals encounter in their attempts to create and sustain an impression, see Erving Goffman, *The Presentation of Self in Everyday Life* (Garden City: Doubleday, 1959).

9. Morton Deutsch and Mary E. Collins, *Interracial Housing* (Minneapolis: University of Minnesota Press, 1951), p. 99.

10. Robert K. Merton, *Social Theory and Social Structure,* rev. ed. (Glencoe: The Free Press, 1957), pp. 319ff.

11. George C. Homans, *The Human Group* (New York: Harcourt, Brace, 1950). See, also, Henry W. Riecken and George C. Homans, "Psychological Aspects of Social Structure," in Gardner Lindzey (ed.), *Handbook of Social Psychology,* Vol. 2 (Cambridge: Addison-Wesley, 1954) pp. 786–832.

12. J. Mayone Stycos, *Family and Fertility in Puerto Rico* (New York: Columbia University Press, 1955), p. 268, *n.* 8; p. 290.

13. Alvin W. Gouldner, "The Norm of Reciprocity: A Preliminary Statement," *American Sociological Review,* Vol. 25 (April 1960), p. 177.

14. For a review of such studies, see Daniel M. Wilner, Rosabelle P. Walkley, and Stuart W. Cook, *Human Relations in Interracial Housing* (Minneapolis: University of Minnesota Press, 1955), pp. 155–63.

15. Deutsch and Collins, *op. cit.*, pp. 55–58.

16. Homans, *op. cit.*, p. 133. For references to other studies which bear out this point, see Riecken and Homans, *op. cit.*, p. 794.

17. See Stuart W. Cook and Claire Selltiz, "Some Factors Which Influence the Attitudinal Outcomes of Personal Contact," *International Social Science Bulletin*, (Vol. 7), 1955, pp. 51–58. For a delineation of elements in the contact situation which are believed to affect the formation of friendships, see Edward A. Suchman, John P. Dean, and Robin M. Williams, Jr., *Desegregation: Some Propositions and Research Suggestions* (New York: Anti-Defamation League of B'nai B'rith, 1958), Chap. 4. Also of interest are the findings of a study in Elmira dealing with Jewish-Gentile relations. It is shown that Jews and Gentiles who have contact within an organization or work situation are more apt to socialize with each other eventually than are those who have contact in a neighborhood setting. John P. Dean, "Jewish Participation in the Life of Middle-Sized American Communities," in Marshall Sklare (ed.), *The Jews* (Glencoe: The Free Press, 1958), pp. 314, 315.

18. Eliot Slater and Moya Woodside, *Patterns of Marriage: A Study of Marriage Relationships in the Urban Working Classes* (London: Cassell, 1951), pp. 100, 101.

19. Burgess and Wallin, *op. cit.*, pp. 238, 404.

20. For an overview of previous research bearing upon this general topic (the relationship between personality indicators and underlying characteristics) and remarks to the effect that much work remains to be done, see Jerome S. Bruner and Renato Tagiuri, "The Perception of People," in Gardner Lindzey (ed.), *Handbook of Social Psychology*, Vol. 2 (Cambridge: Addison-Wesley, 1954), pp. 634–54. See, also, the more recent volume on *Person Perception and Interpersonal Behavior*, edited by Renato Tagiuri and Luigi Petrullo (Stanford: Stanford University Press, 1958), which contains a number of relevant contributions. For a case study of the conditions which led a public figure (Kate Smith) to be regarded as "sincere," see Robert K. Merton, *Mass Persuasion* (New York: Harper, 1946), pp. 76–96 *et passim*.

21. For example, Theodore M. Newcomb, "The Prediction of Interpersonal Attraction," *The American Psychologist*, Vol. 11 (November 1956), pp. 575–86; Renato Tagiuri, Jerome S. Bruner, and Robert R. Blake, "On the Relation between Feelings and Perception of Feelings among Members of Small Groups," in Eleanor E. Maccoby, Theodore M. Newcomb, and Eugene L. Hartley (eds.), *Readings in Social Psychology* (New York: Henry Holt, 1958), pp. 110–16.

22. Cited in Ernest W. Burgess and Harvey J. Locke, *The Family*, 2nd ed. (New York: American Book, 1953), p. 368. See, also, Ira L. Reiss, "Toward a Sociology of the Heterosexual Love Relationship," *Marriage and Family Living* (May 1960), p. 142.

CHAPTER 5

1. "Factors Influencing Change of Occupational Choice," in Paul F. Lazarsfeld and Morris Rosenberg (eds.), *The Language of Social Research* (Glencoe: The Free Press, 1955), p. 256.

2. Robert E. T. Roberts, *Negro-White Intermarriage: A Study of Social Control* (M.A. thesis, University of Chicago, 1940), p. 82.

3. Clifford Kirkpatrick and Theodore Caplow, "*Courtship in a Group of Minnesota Students*," in Robert F. Winch and Robert McGinnis (eds.), *Marriage and The Family* (New York: Henry Holt, 1953), p. 393.

4. For empirical data, see *ibid.*, p. 394.

5. Willard Waller, *The Family*, revised by Reuben Hill (New York: Dryden, 1951), p. 181.

6. Anselm Strauss, *Mirrors and Masks: The Search for Identity* (Glencoe: The Free Press, 1959), Chap. 4.

CHAPTER 6

1. Bernard R. Berelson, Paul F. Lazarsfeld, and William N. McPhee, *Voting* (Chicago: University of Chicago Press, 1954), pp. 98–101. Data on intermarriage collected by the Swiss census would seem to provide another illustration of the "breakage" effect. The figures reveal that children of Protestant-Catholic marriages usually follow the faith that is dominant in their locality. That is, if the canton is predominantly Protestant, then the children are more apt to be Protestant. If the canton is predominantly Catholic, then the children are more likely to follow that faith (Kurt B. Mayer, *The Population of Switzerland* [New York: Columbia University Press, 1952], pp. 185–86).

2. See Judson T. Landis, "Marriages of Mixed and Non-Mixed Religious Faith," *American Sociological Review*, Vol. 14 (June 1949), pp. 401–407; Gerald J. Schnepp, *Leakage From a Catholic Parish* (Washington, D.C.: Catholic University of America Press, 1942), Chap. 4; Board of Social Missions of the United Lutheran Church in America, *A Study of Mixed Marriages in the United Lutheran Church in America*. Incidentally, census data from Switzerland reveal that children of Catholic-Protestant marriages are more apt to be raised in the *father's* religion (whether the father is Catholic or Protestant). See Joseph Candolfi, *Les Mariages Mixtes en Suisse* (Thèse, Publications de l'Institut de Théologie Pastorale de l'Université de Fribourg, Suisse, 1951), pp. 112–14.

3. For an illustration of this phenomenon in an experimental situation, see S. E. Asch, "Effects of Group Pressure upon the Modification and Distortion of Judgments," in Eleanor E. Maccoby, Theodore M. Newcomb, and Eugene L. Hartley (eds.), *Readings in Social Psychology*, New York: Henry Holt, 1958), pp. 174–83.

4. Willard Waller, *The Family*, revised by Reuben Hill (New York: Dryden, 1951, pp. 190–92.

CHAPTER 7

1. For data to the effect that the parent-child relationship actually becomes less harmonious when the child marries someone of a dissimilar socio-cultural background, see Marvin B. Sussman, "Family Continuity: Selective Factors Which Affect Relationships Between Families at Generational Levels," *Marriage and Family Living*, Vol. 16 (May 1954), pp. 112–20.

CHAPTER 8

1. For a discussion of certain mechanisms that speed up the emancipation of the male, see Mirra Komarovsky, "Functional Analysis of Sex Roles," *American Sociological Review*, Vol. 15 (August 1950), pp. 508–16.

2. Evelyn M. Duvall, *In-laws: Pro and Con* (New York: Association Press, 1954), p. 162.

3. For a situation in which indirection is typically employed, see the chapter (by the editors of *Fortune*) on the firing of executives in *The Executive Life* (Garden City: Doubleday, 1956), pp. 179–94.

4. William J. Goode, *After Divorce* (Glencoe: The Free Press, 1956), p. 82.

5. *Ibid.*, p. 83. That these results were an artifact of the wife's reporting is further suggested by a finding from the study by Ernest W. Burgess and Paul Wallin of 1,000 engaged couples. Practically no difference was found in the percentage of men's and women's parents who disapproved of the forthcoming marriage. (*Engagement and Marriage*, [Chicago: Lippincott, 1953] p. 561.)

CHAPTER 9

1. Robert K. Merton, *Social Theory and Social Structure*, rev. ed. (Glencoe: The Free Press, 1957), p. 374.

2. See Gresham M. Sykes and David Matza, "Techniques of Neutralization: A Theory of Delinquency," *American Sociological Review*, Vol. 22 (December 1957), pp. 664–70.

3. *Ibid.*, p. 668. Merton has discussed the widespread tendency, in the contemporary scene, for individuals and groups to question the sources from which the thought and conduct of others derive. See Robert K. Merton, *op. cit.*, pp. 457–59.

CHAPTER 10

1. For empirical data on this point, see John E. Mayer, "The Self-Restraint of Friends: A Mechanism in Family Transition," *Social Forces*, Vol. 35 (March 1957), pp. 230–38.

2. See, for example, Bernard R. Berelson, Paul F. Lazarsfeld, and William N. McPhee, *Voting* (Chicago: University of Chicago Press, 1954), Chap. 6.

3. "Friendship as Social Process: A Substantive and Methodological Analysis," in Morroe Berger, Theodore Abel, and Charles H. Page (eds.), *Freedom and Control in Modern Society* (Toronto: Van Nostrand, 1954), pp. 18–66.

CHAPTER 11

1. For a study of intermarriage which is more psychologically oriented than the present one, see Maria H. Levinson and Daniel J. Levinson, "Jews

Who Intermarry: Sociopsychological Bases of Ethnic Identity and Change," *Yivo Annual of Jewish Social Science,* Vol. 12 (1958–1959), pp. 103–30.

2. Willard Waller, *The Family,* revised by Reuben Hill (New York: Dryden, 1951), p. 364.

Index